W9-BRZ-871

Chicago Public Library

REFERENCE

Form 178 rev. 11-00

The Middle East

Volume 4
QATAR • SAUDI ARABIA • SYRIA

Titles in the series

Volume 1
BAHRAIN • CYPRUS • EGYPT

Volume 2
IRAN • IRAQ • ISRAEL

Volume 3
JORDAN • KUWAIT • LEBANON • OMAN

Volume 4
QATAR • SAUDI ARABIA • SYRIA

Volume 5
TURKEY • UNITED ARAB EMIRATES • YEMEN

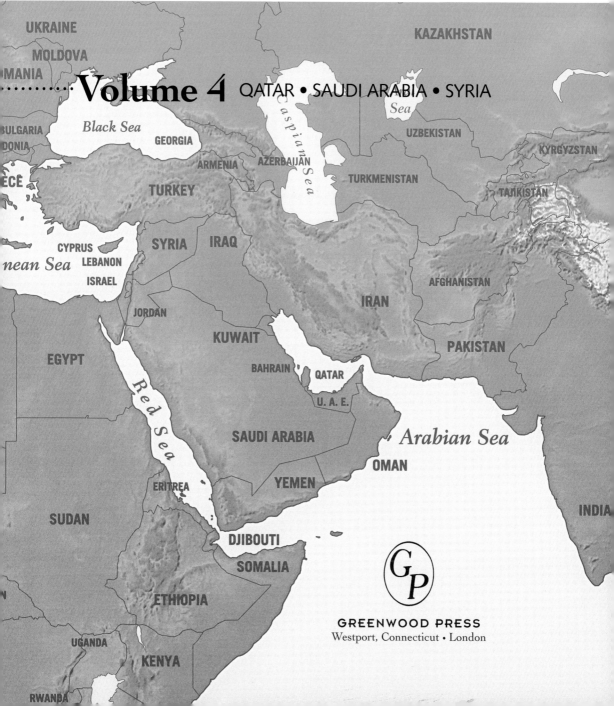

Discovering
World Cultures

The Middle East

Volume 4 QATAR • SAUDI ARABIA • SYRIA

GREENWOOD PRESS
Westport, Connecticut • London

Library of Congress Cataloging-in-Publication Data

Discovering world cultures: the Middle East / by Creative Media Applications.
        p. cm. — (Middle school reference)
        Contents: v. 1. Bahrain, Cyprus, Egypt — v. 2. Iran, Iraq, Israel — v. 3. Jordan, Kuwait, Lebanon,
    Oman — v. 4. Qatar, Saudi Arabia, Syria — v. 5. Turkey, United Arab Emirates, Yemen.
        Includes bibliographical references and index.
        ISBN 0–313–32922–2 (set: alk. paper)—ISBN 0–313–32923–0 (v. 1: alk.paper)—
        ISBN 0–313–32924–9 (v. 2: alk. paper)—ISBN 0–313–32925–7 (v. 3: alk. paper)—
        ISBN 0–313–32926–5 (v. 4: alk. paper)—ISBN 0–313–32927–3 (v. 5: alk. paper)
           1. Ethnology — Middle East. 2. Middle East — Social life and customs. I. Creative Media Applications.
           II. Series.
        GN635.N42D57   2004
        306.'0956 — dc22   2003044263

British Library Cataloguing in Publication Data is available.

Library of Congress Catalog Card Number: 2003044263
ISBN: 0–313–32922–2 (set)
        0–313–32923–0 (vol. 1)
        0–313–32924–9 (vol. 2)
        0–313–32925–7 (vol. 3)
        0–313–32926–5 (vol. 4)
        0–313–32927–3 (vol. 5)

First published in 2004

Greenwood Press, 88 Post Road West, Westport, CT 06881
An imprint of Greenwood Publishing Group, Inc.
www.greenwood.com

Printed in the United States of America

∞™

The paper used in this book complies with the Permanent Paper Standard
issued by the National Information Standards Organization (Z39.48–1984).

10 9 8 7 6 5 4 3 2 1

A Creative Media Applications, Inc. Production
WRITER: Sandy Pobst
DESIGN AND PRODUCTION: Alan Barnett, Inc.
EDITOR: Susan Madoff
COPYEDITOR: Laurie Lieb
PROOFREADER: Betty Pessagno
INDEXER: Nara Wood
ASSOCIATED PRESS PHOTO RESEARCHER: Yvette Reyes
CONSULTANT: Abraham Marcus is Associate Professor of Middle Eastern History and
    former Director of the Center for Middle Eastern Studies at the University of Texas at Austin.

PHOTO CREDITS:
AP/Wide World Photographs pages: x, 2, 7, 16, 19, 23, 27, 34, 36, 53, 55, 57, 58, 63, 72, 75, 95
© Arthur Thevenart/CORBIS pages: 3, 90
© Christine Osborne/CORBIS page: 4
© Bettmann/CORBIS pages: 6, 47, 86, 92
© Hulton Archives/Getty Images pages: 9, 48, 88
© REUTERS /Landov pages: 11, 110
© Ali Jarekji/Reuters /Landov pages: 12, 30, 42, 44, 64
© Stuart Clarke/Bloomberg News /Landov page: 14
© Chris Helgren/REUTERS /Landov pages: 15, 21
© Graham Tim/CORBIS SYGMA page: 20
© Tim Aubry/Reuters /Landov page: 25
© Mike Nelson/EPA /Landov pages: 31, 41
© Jeremy Horner/CORBIS page: 33
© Shamil Zhumatov/REUTERS /Landov page: 39, 69
© Wolfgang Kaehler/CORBIS page: 45
© EPA /Landov pages: 61, 82
© Khaled Al-Hariri/Reuters /Landov pages: 76, 79, 81, 96, 98, 101, 103, 115
© Roger Wood/CORBIS pages: 83, 113
© Vanni Archive/CORBIS page: 85
© Archivo Iconografico, S.A./CORBIS page: 89
© Jorge Ferrari/EPA /Landov pages: 104, 107, 108

Table of Contents

Special thanks go to Aline Mouchawar, a citizen of Syria and the United States, who graciously shared her knowledge of her native country. Mary Ann Segalla and Amy Snyder contributed to this volume.

INTRODUCTION

The Middle East. The name conjures up many different images for most Westerners: fascinating ancient civilizations, the rise and fall of powerful empires, and—most recently—bloody conflicts and suicide bombers. This series introduces the history, customs, and cultures of the people living in the Middle East in the hope of inspiring a fuller understanding of a complex region.

What Is the Middle East?

"The Middle East" is a rather vague name for such an important region of the world. What is it in the middle of? And how is it different from the Near East and the Far East?

Most of the geographical terms used in the world today, such as the label "Middle East," originated with Europeans and Americans. As Europeans explored the world around them, they first headed east. The lands that bordered the eastern basin of the Mediterranean Sea—Anatolia (Turkey), Syria, Palestine, and Egypt, as well as their immediate neighbors—became known as the "Near East." Countries farther away, such as China and Indonesia, were referred to as the "Far East."

The term "Middle East" has been in use for only the past century. It was first used by an American military officer to describe the geopolitical

MEASURING TIME

Most of the world today uses the Gregorian calendar, which is based on the solar year. Because it is a Christian calendar, historical dates have traditionally been designated as occurring before the birth of Christ (B.C.) or after the birth of Christ (A.D., an acronym for the Latin phrase *Anno Domini,* meaning "in the year of the Lord"). In recent years, historians have started to use neutral, nonreligious terms to describe these divisions of time. The *Discovering World Cultures: The Middle East* series follows this practice, using B.C.E. (before the Common Era) rather than B.C. and C.E. (Common Era) in place of A.D. (Some people define the terms as "Before the Christian Era" and "Christian Era.") The dating system remains the same: 1000 B.C. is the same as 1000 B.C.E., while 2003 C.E. is the same as A.D. 2003.

region that included the countries between the Mediterranean Sea and India—those countries in the middle of the Eastern Hemisphere that shared a common culture. Today, there are many different definitions of the Middle East. Some scholars include the countries of northern Africa in their definition of the Middle East. Others use a cultural definition that includes all the predominantly Islamic countries in Africa and Asia. This series adopts the definition used by most modern scholars, adding Egypt to the original list of Middle Eastern countries because of its shared history and Arabic culture.

Birthplace of World Religions

As home to the world's earliest civilizations, the Middle East is also the birthplace of three of the world's major religions: Judaism, Christianity, and Islam. Followers of these three religions worship the same god and share a common early history. Today, about 2 billion people worldwide identify themselves as Christian, while about 1.3 billion follow Islam. Nearly 14 million are Jews. Together, these three groups make up 53 percent of the world's population.

Judaism

Judaism is the oldest of the three religions, originating nearly 4,000 years ago in the land of Israel (also known as Palestine). Jews believe that Abraham, who was born in Ur in present-day Iraq, was the founder of Judaism. About 1800 B.C.E., he began to teach that the world was created by a single god. God made a covenant, or agreement, with Abraham: if Abraham left his home and followed God's commandments, God would bless Abraham with children and establish a great nation. Moses, a descendant of Abraham's son Isaac, later led the Jewish people out of slavery in Egypt. God made a new covenant with Moses, providing instructions and rules for living a holy life, including the Ten Commandments.

According to Jewish tradition, Abraham's first son, Ishmael, is the ancestor of the Arab people. His second son, Isaac, is the ancestor of the Jewish people.

Jews believe that when they follow the Torah—the first five books of the Hebrew Bible, or holy book—and keep God's laws, the Jewish people and the nation of Israel will be blessed by God. They also believe that God will send a Messiah, a political leader chosen by God to bring the

Jewish *exiles* back to Israel, rebuild Jerusalem and restore the Temple that was destroyed by the Romans in 70 C.E., and put an end to the evil in the world. (For more information about Judaism, please see page 108 in Volume 2.)

Christianity

Christianity grew out of Judaism about 2,000 years ago in Israel when Jesus Christ, a Jewish man, began teaching about faith and God's love. Christians believe that Jesus Christ is the son of God, the Messiah sent by God to save people from sin and death. They believe that Jesus was resurrected after his death and that, through faith, they too will have life after death. The Christian Bible includes both the Hebrew Bible (Old Testament) and the teachings of Jesus and his disciples (the New Testament). Unlike Jews and Muslims, Christians believe in the Trinity of God—that God exists as the Father, the Son, and the Holy Spirit. (For more information about Christianity, please see pages 56–60 in Volume 1 of *Discovering World Cultures: The Middle East*.)

Islam

Islam was founded in the seventh century by the Prophet Mohammad, who was a direct descendant of Ishmael. Muslims believe in only one god, Allah, the same god worshiped by Jews and Christians. According to Islamic tradition, Allah's message to humans has been delivered by prophets, such as Abraham, Moses, Jesus, and Mohammad. Holy books, including the Torah, the Christian Gospels, and the Qur'an, preserve the word of Allah. Because the countries in the Middle East are predominantly Islamic, a detailed overview of Islam is provided here.

Basic Beliefs

Muslims believe that the "five pillars of Islam" are the key to salvation:

- *Shahadah*: the acknowledgment that "there is no god but God and that Mohammad is the messenger of God"
- *Salah*: five daily ritual prayers
- *Zakat*: the giving of money to the poor
- *Sawm*: the dawn-to-dusk fast during the month of Ramadan, Islam's most important religious observance
- *Hajj*: the pilgrimage to Mecca, the birthplace of Mohammad

Forms of Islam

About 85 percent of the Islamic community follows the Sunni tradition (in Arabic, *Sunni* refers to the people who follow the sunna, or example, of the prophet). Sunni Muslims believe that the *caliph,* or spiritual leader, should be chosen by the consensus of the Islamic community. They also believe that following *shari'a,* or Islamic, law is essential in living a life that ends in salvation.

The Shi'a tradition teaches that Mohammad appointed his cousin and son-in-law Ali and his descendants to be the spiritual and worldly leaders of Islam after Mohammad's death. Shi'ite (SHE-ite) Muslims believe that these leaders, called *imams,* are free of sin and infallible. About 15 percent of all Muslims follow Shi'a Islam, but there are several different branches within the Shi'a tradition.

Wahhabism is an Islamic reform movement that originated in the eighteenth century in Saudi Arabia. Its members are the most conservative, fundamentalist group in Islam. Members reject any

Iraqi Shi'ite Muslims gather at a holy site in the city of Karbala, Iraq, in April 2003, to mourn the death of one of their most important saints. Under the rule of Iraqi leader Saddam Hussein, they had been banned from observing such rituals for decades. With Hussein's fall from power that same month, however, they were free to worship.

modern interpretations of Islam, including the celebration of Mohammad's birthday or playing music. Muslims who adopt Wahhabi principles label those who don't share their beliefs as infidels or unbelievers, even those who are moderate Sunnis and Shi'ites.

Sources of Muslim Teachings and Tradition

The Qur'an is the only holy book of the Islam faith. Muslims believe that the Qur'an contains the literal word of Allah, or God, which was revealed to the Prophet Mohammad. Memorizing and reciting these holy words is an important part of daily prayer and worship. (Many Americans refer to this book as the Koran, a Westernized spelling of Qur'an.)

While the Qur'an is the only holy text, there are other important spiritual sources in the Islamic faith. The Sunna is a collection of all the stories, sayings, and actions of Mohammad. Followers of Islam use these examples to determine correct behavior in areas not covered in the Qur'an. They often come up with different explanations, which is why customs and beliefs vary sometimes from group to group. One of the distinct features of Islam is the Shari'a, a comprehensive body of laws covering personal, civil, and criminal matters.

COURTESY AND CUSTOMS IN THE MIDDLE EAST

Middle Eastern customs and traditions have developed over centuries, influenced by tribal culture and religion. Visitors to the region should be aware of rules and taboos, such as the ones shown here, that apply in most Middle Eastern countries.

- When greeting a man, clasp his hand briefly without shaking it. A man should never move to shake hands with a woman unless she offers her hand first. Inquiries about an acquaintance's health and interests are expected, but you should never ask about a Muslim's female family members.

- Showing the sole of your shoe to another person, such as when you sit with one leg crossed over the other knee, is very rude. The soles of your shoes should always be pointing downward.

- Always offer and receive items with your right hand. If you are served a meal in a traditional manner, use your right hand for eating (the left hand is regarded as unclean).

- When you visit a person's home, compliments about the home are welcome, but avoid admiring or praising an item excessively. The host may feel obligated to give the item to you as a gift.

- Photographing people is viewed with suspicion in some areas. It is important to ask permission before photographing anyone, especially a woman.

Major Religious Holidays

- *Ashura:* The first ten days of the New Year are a period of mourning for Shi'ite Muslims as they remember the assassination of Hussein, grandson of the Prophet Mohammad, in 680 C.E.

- *Ramadan:* Ramadan honors the time when Mohammad received the first of the Qur'an from Allah. It is the ninth and most holy month in the Islamic year. Muslims do not eat or drink from dawn until dusk during Ramadan. Instead, they reflect on their relationship with Allah, asking for forgiveness for their sins.

- *Eid al-Fitr:* As Ramadan ends, Muslims gather with family and friends to celebrate the feast of Eid al-Fitr. Children often get new clothes for the holiday, which usually lasts three days. Gifts are exchanged among friends and family.

- *Eid al-Adha:* Eid al-Adha (the Feast of the Sacrifice) honors the Prophet Abraham and his devotion to God. At the end of the hajj, the pilgrimage to Mecca, an animal is sacrificed, and the meat is divided between family members and the poor.

A Final Note

Transcribing the Arabic language into English often creates confusion. The two alphabets are very different and there is not a direct correlation of sounds. As a result, Arabic words are often given several different spellings in Western writing. One source may refer to the *emir* of a region, while another labels the ruler an *amir*. The name of the prophet who established Islam appears as Mohammad, Muhammad, and Mohammed. The Islamic holy book is the Qur'an or Koran, and so on. Another source of confusion is the different place names used by Westerners and those who live in the Middle East. For instance, the body of water between Iraq and the Arabian Peninsula has been called the Persian Gulf for centuries by Westerners. People living nearby, however, refer to it as the Arabian Gulf. In this series, the most commonly used spellings and the labels most familiar to Westerners have been used in an effort to avoid confusion. The exception lies in the spelling of *Qur'an,* the Islamic holy book, since scholars as well as many Muslims prefer that spelling over the Westernized *Koran.*

Qatar

One of the least well-known countries in the Middle East, Qatar (KAH-ter) leaped into the American consciousness in 2003 when the war on Iraq was directed from the small Persian Gulf country. After years of increasingly corrupt rule and limitations on civil rights, Sheikh Hamad bin Khalifa Al Thani took control of the government. Today, Qatar has gained a reputation as one of the most moderate and democratic countries in the region despite its adherence to Wahhabism, one of the strictest forms of Islam.

The Qataris

The Qatari people are descendants of Arabs who migrated from the central Arabian Peninsula in the eighteenth century. They belonged to nomadic tribes that raised camels and other livestock. Over time, some settled in villages near the coast and relied upon fishing, pearling, and trading for their income.

Following World War II (1939–1945), oil production boomed. Workers from other countries immigrated to Qatar and found employment in the petroleum industry. Today, these foreign residents make up over 75 percent of the population. Most are from Pakistan, India, and Iran, although a number of Arabs from other countries are employed in Qatar as well.

Did You Know?

Arabic is written from right to left. The Arabic alphabet has twenty-eight letters, three of which serve as consonants and vowels.

FAST FACTS

✔ **Official name:** State of Qatar

✔ **Capital:** Doha

✔ **Location:** Eastern coast of the Arabian Peninsula

✔ **Area:** 4,416 square miles (11,437 square kilometers)

✔ **Population:** 793,341 (July 2002 estimate)

✔ **Age distribution:**
0–14 years: 25%
15–64 years: 72%
over 65 years: 3%

✔ **Life expectancy:**
Males: 70 years
Females: 75 years

✔ **Ethnic groups:** Arab 40%, Pakistani 18%, Indian 18%, Iranian 10%, other 14%

✔ **Religions:** Muslim 95%, other 5%

✔ **Languages:** Arabic (official), Urdu, English

✔ **Currency:**
Qatari rial (QAR)
US$1 = 3.64 QAR (7/03)

✔ **Average annual income:** US$18,800

✔ **Major exports:** Oil, gas

Source: CIA, *The World Factbook 2002;* BBC News Country Profiles.

Arabic is the official language in Qatar, but English and Urdu are widely spoken as well.

Land and Resources

Located on the eastern coast of the Arabian Peninsula, Qatar itself is a small peninsula that juts into the Persian Gulf. The Qatari peninsula measures about 100 miles (160 kilometers) from north to south and 56 miles (90 kilometers) at its widest point. It covers about 4,416 square miles (11,437 square kilometers), making it slightly smaller than Connecticut. Qatar's southern land borders are shared with Saudi Arabia and the United Arab Emirates.

Geography

Qatar's rocky landscape is nearly flat, with the highest point measuring only 130 feet (40 meters) above sea level. In the southeastern region an inlet known as Khawr al-Udayd, or the Inland Sea, is surrounded by gigantic sand dunes. Salt pans—natural depressions where water accumulates

The landscape of tiny Qatar is flat and rocky. Along its coast are salt pans, where seawater accumulates and then evaporates, leaving salt deposits behind. This salt pan is located on the east coast of Qatar, near Doha, the nation's capital.

before evaporating and leaving salty deposits—are found in several areas, primarily along the coast. The largest salt pan is located along the southeastern coast. A long limestone ridge follows the southwestern coastline and marks the location of Qatar's first oil field, the Dukhan Field.

Qatar claims several of the islands that lie off its coastline. The most important is Halul Island, near the capital city of Doha. Oil loading terminals on the island serve the offshore oil fields. The Hawar Islands, off Qatar's west coast, were claimed by both Qatar and Bahrain for decades. In 2001, however, the International Court of Justice at The Hague ruled that the islands belonged to Bahrain.

Major Cities

The capital city of Doha, located on the east coast, is the largest urban area in Qatar with 75 percent of the population. Until oil production began in 1949, however, Doha was a small village dependent upon the fishing and pearling industries. Today, it is a modern city, with an international airport, seaport, and attractions such as the Aladdin's Kingdom theme park. Fishing remains an important industry in the area.

Doha is located on the east coast and is the largest urban area in Qatar, with 75 percent of the nation's population. Situated on the Persian Gulf, Doha is also the nation's chief port.

Climate

Qatar has a desert climate, with extremely hot summers and mild winters. From June through September, temperatures often soar above 131° F (55° C). High levels of humidity combine with the extreme temperatures to produce a sauna-like effect. By November, temperatures have dropped to more comfortable levels, although they rarely fall below 62° F (17° C).

Rain rarely falls on the peninsula; Qatar averages less than 4 inches (10 centimeters) of precipitation annually. Most of this falls during short, but intense, winter storms. The sudden cloudbursts often result in flash floods as water races through the usually dry ravines and *wadis* (generally dry riverbeds).

Sand and dust storms are a common occurrence in the spring and winter. These can be very dangerous, completely obscuring the view and causing damage to buildings. At times, the dust is so thick that air and road traffic is halted until the storm ends.

Natural Resources

The Qatar Peninsula is rocky and largely barren, with little water. The little underground water that is accessible is of little use for drinking or agricultural irrigation due to its high mineral levels. Until *desalination* technology enabled Qatar to convert seawater into drinking water, the number of people who could live in the region was limited.

Qatar's greatest natural resources are the large deposits of oil and natural gas that have made Qatar one of the wealthiest countries in the world. The inland oil fields were the first to be discovered, but the natural gas reservoir discovered just off Qatar's north coast—called the North Field—promises to be the most important in the long term. Experts believe that the North Field, estimated to be the largest natural gas reservoir in the world, holds a 200-year supply of natural gas. (The oil fields are expected to produce oil for only twenty-five more years.)

> **Did You Know?**
>
> The North Field holds an estimated 386 trillion tons (350 trillion metric tons) of natural gas. In practical terms, that much gas could heat all the homes in the United States for sixty years.

Plants and Animals

The dry, rocky desert and extreme climate of Qatar are inhospitable to plant life, leaving most of the peninsula barren. Few animals other than birds or bats make their home in Qatar.

History

Ancient Days

For centuries, nomadic tribes from present-day Saudi Arabia traveled across the Qatari Peninsula with their livestock, camping at the few freshwater sources. Small settlements grew up along the eastern coast, where fishing and pearling provided food and income for inhabitants.

The Conquerors

The Arab tribes that roamed across Qatar were among the first to adopt Islam after the Prophet Mohammad introduced the new religion in the seventh century. Islam soon spread to the settlements on the Qatari coastline, and the region was considered part of the Islamic realm with leadership in the hands of the *caliphs*—religious and political leaders who ruled after Mohammad's death. Under the rule of the Abbasid caliphs (750–1258 C.E.), new settlements were established on Qatar.

Sultan Abdul Hamid II, pictured here, was the ruler of the Ottoman Empire, based in Turkey, from 1876 to 1909. The Ottoman Empire spread eastward toward the end of the nineteenth century, and Qatar came under its control in 1872.

IMPORTANT EVENTS IN QATAR'S HISTORY

48000 B.C.E.	Stone Age people settle along Qatar's coast.
5000 B.C.E.	Mesopotamian and Arabic cultures flourish in Qatar.
610 C.E.	The Prophet Mohammad receives revelations from God and begins preaching the religion of Islam, which means "surrender to God."
7th century	Islam spreads to the Qatari Peninsula.
1760s	The Al Khalifa and Al Jalahima families of the Bani Utub tribe arrive in Qatar.
1783	The Al Khalifa take control of Bahrain, and most members of the family move there.
1820	The British negotiate the General Treaty of Peace with Persian Gulf rulers, hoping to end attacks on British ships.
1868	Britain recognizes Qatar as a separate nation from Bahrain. The new treaty establishes the Al Thani family as the rulers of Qatar.
1872	The Ottoman Empire expands to include Qatar.
1913	Ottoman control officially ends.
1916	Qatar becomes a British *protectorate*.
1930s	Most Qataris relocate in other countries following the collapse of the pearling industry and the worldwide economic depression.
1935	Qatar grants Britain the right to explore for oil.
1939	Anglo-Persian Oil Company discovers oil near present-day Dukhan. World War II breaks out, delaying production.

1949	Oil exports begin. Foreigners flock to Qatar in search of well-paying jobs.
1956	Qataris protest Britain's role in their government as well as the extravagances of the emir.
1960	Sheikh Ahmad bin Ali becomes emir. His cousin, Sheikh Khalifa bin Hamad, assumes most of the day-to-day responsibilities of governing.
1963	The National Unity Front forms, calling for more social services and the recognition of trade unions.
1971	Britain grants Qatar its independence.
1972	While Ahmad is out of the country, Khalifa takes control of the government and declares himself emir.
1974	The Qatari government announces the formation of the Qatar General Petroleum Corporation, which takes over all oil operations from the Anglo-Persian Oil Company.
1993	Qatar establishes diplomatic relations with Iran and Israel.
1995	Sheikh Hamad bin Khalifa wrests control of the government away from his father.
1999	Qataris—both men and women—vote in democratic municipal elections for the first time.
2002	Qatar allows the United States to establish command bases on the peninsula in preparation for war with Iraq.

In the mid-eighteenth century, the Al Khalifa and Al Jalahima families of the Bani Utub tribe arrived in Qatar from Kuwait. They settled along the northwest coast, establishing the city of az-Zubarah. Oyster beds along the coast helped the Al Khalifa and Al Jalahima develop a successful pearling industry, building upon their trading ties with Kuwait.

The Al Khalifa and Al Jalahima had historically competed against one another for wealth and power. In 1783, the Al Khalifa gained control of the island of Bahrain. Bahrain was a rich prize; its trade with Asia and the Middle East brought many people and goods into its ports. Over time, most of the Al Khalifa moved from Qatar to Bahrain, where they continue to rule today. The Al Jalahima, resentful of the Al Khalifa's claim to Bahrain, began launching attacks on Bahraini ships at sea. They soon gained a fearsome reputation as pirates.

New Influences

The British arrived in the Persian Gulf region in the late eighteenth century. The East India Company had established trading centers in India. As they began to ship more goods to England, Britain became concerned for the safety of the ships. As a result, the General Treaty of Peace of 1820 was negotiated with the sheikhs (shayks), or rulers, along the Persian Gulf coast. This agreement established British authority in the Gulf in an effort to end pirate attacks on British ships.

Did You Know?

The southeastern coast of the Arabian Peninsula became known as the Trucial Coast rather than the Pirate Coast following treaty negotiations that established a truce between Britain and the area's sheikhs.

Until 1868, most other nations considered Qatar a dependency of Bahrain. After a series of pirate attacks on British ships off the coast of Qatar, however, the British negotiated treaties with both Bahrain and Qatar, recognizing them as separate entities. Muhammad bin Thani bin Muhammad acted as the representative of the Qatari tribes, establishing the Al Thani family as the rulers of Qatar. (The Al Thani tribe is believed to have migrated from central Arabia during the same period as the Al Khalifa and Al Jalahima, but little is known about its history prior to this treaty.)

The Ottoman Empire expanded into the Arabian Peninsula in the late nineteenth century, bringing Qatar under its control. Although the Ottomans officially ruled over Qatar from 1872 until 1913, they held little real power after the turn of the century, due to the ongoing resistance of Sheikh Qasim bin Muhammad Al Thani and his supporters.

In 1916, following the end of Ottoman rule, the Al Thani negotiated a treaty with Britain that made Qatar a British *protectorate*. This meant that Britain would provide military protection for Qatar in return for the right to oversee Qatar's foreign affairs. For over a decade, however, little assistance was given to Qatar's *emir* (ruler) when competing tribes and family members threatened his leadership. Compounding the problem was the collapse of the pearling industry in the late 1920s and the worldwide economic depression of the 1930s. Many Qataris, faced with food shortages and unemployment, left the country and didn't return until the end of World War II (1939–1945).

Wealth and Discontent

When oil was discovered in the Persian Gulf area in the 1930s, Britain eagerly renegotiated its treaty with Qatar, offering the royal family more assistance and protection. In return, the 1935 treaty gave the British-owned Anglo-Persian Oil Company the right to drill for oil in Qatar,

Oil has long been the most important natural resource in the Middle East. This derrick in Iran, owned by the Anglo-Iranian Oil Company, was photographed in 1909. Oil was discovered in Qatar in 1939 by the newly established Anglo-Persian Oil Company.

effectively preventing American companies from gaining a foothold in the country.

Oil was discovered in Qatar in 1939, just as World War II began. Because of the war, oil production did not reach its height until the late 1940s. Before long, oil revenues were mounting, and so were Emir Abdullah bin Qasim's problems. Much of the oil income was distributed among the royal family, but many relatives rebelled against the emir, demanding a larger share. In 1949, the emir invited the British to establish an official presence in Qatar—including a police force—in return for supporting his son, Ali bin Abdullah, as the new ruler.

Over the next decade, a new government was founded under the guidance of the British. Telephone networks, desalination plants, electrical power plants, and airstrips were built, establishing the *infrastructure* of modern Qatar. Thousands of immigrants from other Arab countries and southwest Asia arrived to work in the oil industry.

Although many gains were made during this period, many Qataris remained poor. Those who were not in the Al Thani family, as well as distant relatives of the emir who received only small allowances, became increasingly discontented with the status quo. In 1956, over 2,000 Qataris marched through the streets of Doha to protest the emir's policies and the presence of the British. The emir strengthened the police force after the protest march, but didn't change any of his policies. Rather, he continued to spend freely on extravagances such as his villa in Switzerland and hunting trips to Pakistan, even as oil revenues declined.

In 1960, the emir stepped down, naming his son, Ahmad bin Ali, as the new ruler of Qatar. One of Ahmad bin Ali's first actions was to take money that had been spent on public works projects and distribute it among the royal family.

Resentment against the new emir grew, and in 1963, the National Unity Front was formed. This group called for Qatari workers to strike in protest against the emir's policies. Among the workers' demands were increased social services, reduced privileges for the ruling class, and the recognition of trade unions. Ahmad bin Ali responded by arresting and exiling the leaders of the movement.

Ahmad bin Ali, like his father, spent much of his time traveling outside the country. In his absence, Khalifa bin Hamad took over much of the government's operation, quietly building the country's infrastructure along with his own political power base.

Independence

In the late 1960s, Britain announced that it would be ending its protectorate system in the Gulf region in 1971. Qatar, Bahrain, and the Trucial States (present-day United Arab Emirates) considered forming a federated nation, but the less prosperous countries feared that Bahrain would dominate the union. When the British withdrew in September 1971, Ahmad bin Ali announced Qatar's new status as an independent Islamic nation.

Dissatisfaction with Ahmad bin Ali reached a critical point after he announced Qatar's independence from his residence in Switzerland. Six months after independence, Khalifa bin Hamad—with the approval of most Qataris, including the Al Thani, and the support of Britain and Saudi Arabia—took over control of the government and declared himself emir.

Emir Khalifa bin Hamad was photographed on June 23, 1995, as he traveled to Geneva, Switzerland. Four days later, his son, Sheikh Hamad, seized control of the Qatari government while his father was away.

In the early years of Khalifa bin Hamad's rule, he made several changes that improved the lives of many Qataris. After reducing the money given to members of the royal family, he increased funding for education, health care, and other social services. The Qatar General Petroleum Corporation was formed in 1974, taking over all oil operations from the British-owned Anglo-Persian Oil Company.

Over time, however, the emir shifted an estimated $3 to $7 billion of oil and gas revenues to his private bank accounts. The government aligned itself with Saudi Arabia, to the extent that the Saudi government controlled much of Qatar's foreign policy. Freedom of speech was strictly curtailed, and anyone who criticized the government was swiftly punished.

In the early 1990s, as the emir's son—Sheikh Hamad—began taking on more responsibility, Saudi Arabia's influence on Qatar's foreign policy began to shrink. His open relations with Iran caused consternation in

After seizing power in 1995, Sheikh Hamad, pictured here in June 2003, implemented governmental reforms that encourage democracy in Qatar. Under Sheikh Hamad, Qatar has also become an important ally in the Middle East for the United States.

the Persian Gulf region, where most of the monarchs viewed Iran's fundamentalist *theocracy* (religion-driven government) as a threat to their own existence. Qatar's diplomatic contact with Israel in 1993, as well as an agreement two years later to export natural gas to Israel, also drew criticism from Arab countries.

Qatar Today

In June 1995, Sheikh Hamad, the son of the emir, took control of the government while his father was out of the country in a *coup* that was supported by members of the royal family and others in the government. His father did not quietly accept the loss of power, however. Within a year, Khalifa attempted to regain the throne three times, without success.

Hamad immediately began reforming the government. One of his first acts was to make it illegal for any ruler to use the nation's oil and gas revenues as personal income. A woman was appointed to serve as the Under-Secretary for Education and Culture, the first time a woman had ever been chosen for a national leadership position. All citizens—men and women—were given the right to run for office and vote in elections. By 1999, democratic municipal elections were held. The government expects to hold a parliamentary election within a few years.

Following the Persian Gulf War (1991), Qatar reconsidered its dependence upon Saudi Arabia for military support and began building stronger ties with the United States. (The Saudis were unable to protect themselves from Iraq during the conflict and had to rely upon military support from the United States and Britain in order to remain independent.) In 1996, the Qatari government spent more than $1 billion to build the Al-Udeid Air Base, at a time when it had no air force. The United States entered negotiations to use the air base, and in 2001, Al-Udeid served as the main base of operations for the U.S. military during the war in Afghanistan. In 2003, the U.S. command center for the war against Iraq was established at As-Sayliyah, a U.S. military base near Doha.

Economy

As the twentieth century began, Qatar was a poor country whose citizens depended upon meager incomes gained from fishing, pearling, and raising livestock. Today, most Qataris work in the oil and gas industries. Only a few continue to follow traditional occupations such as raising camels, sheep, and goats or fishing. Today, because of the quality and size of the oil and gas reserves, Qatar is one of the wealthiest countries in the world.

Business and Industry

Since the mid-twentieth century, Qatar's economy has been based upon revenues from oil and gas production. Today, those revenues make up about 95 percent of the national income. Until recently, most of Qatar's income came from oil. In the late 1980s, however, the world's largest natural gas reserve—known as the North Field—was discovered off the coast of Qatar. Since then, revenues from gas exports have exceeded

Qatar's economy is largely based on oil and natural gas production, but other businesses, such as an international airline, thrive as well. The chief executive of Qatar Airways is pictured in 2002, holding a model of a new aircraft the airline had just purchased.

those from oil. Gas is expected to continue to provide most of Qatar's income in the future.

Aside from the oil and gas industries, Qatar has several small manufacturing industries, including factories that produce cement, fertilizers, petrochemicals, and steel.

Media and Communications

Until the mid-1990s, Qatar's government strictly censored the media. No criticism of the government or the royal family was allowed. When

AL JAZEERA

Al Jazeera, the first independent Arab broadcasting company, was established in Qatar in 1996. Although the network has been supported financially by Emir Hamad since its beginning, Al Jazeera operates free from any government censorship—a rarity in the Arab world. Modeled after the American news network CNN, Al Jazeera presents in-depth programming that often explores sensitive topics, such as human rights in the Middle East, the systematic oppression of women in some Middle Eastern countries, and the acceptance of ancient Islamic codes in today's modern world.

Al Jazeera's popularity soared in 2001, when the United States launched its war against terrorists in Afghanistan. For the first time, Arabs were seeing uncensored footage and commentary from their point of view. After Al Jazeera broadcast audio- and videotapes that purportedly showed known terrorist Osama bin Laden, the United States accused the network of inciting Islamic fundamentalists to action.

Al Jazeera journalists often find themselves in trouble with the governments of countries in which they are working. Jordan, Egypt, and Kuwait have all temporarily closed Al Jazeera news bureaus or restricted its correspondents after programs that disparaged their governments. In 2003, Americans were outraged by Al Jazeera broadcasts that showed American casualties and prisoners of war in Iraq. The New York Stock Exchange responded to the broadcasts by banning Al Jazeera correspondents.

Although initial plans were for Al Jazeera to be self-supporting within five years, the emir has had to provide additional financial support despite the station's immense popularity. The lack of financial support from the business sector is due in large part to Al Jazeera's freedom from censorship. Advertisers, especially multinational firms that do business in Saudi Arabia, have hesitated to buy advertising on the station, given the Saudi government's antagonism toward Al Jazeera. (The Saudis have labeled the station "poisonous" and urged its citizens not to watch.)

The news is monitored from Al Jazeera's control room in Doha, Qatar.

Hamad became emir, he eliminated the official policy of censorship. In 1996, the emir eliminated the state-run Information Ministry and provided start-up financing for Al Jazeera, the first independent Arab television network to provide round-the-clock news and programming.

Religion and Beliefs

Over 95 percent of the population in Qatar, including foreign residents, is Muslim. The Qataris follow Sunni tradition, but they belong to the strict Wahhabi sect that originated in Arabia in the eighteenth century. There is a small Shi'ite population in Qatar, made up primarily of Iranians. Non-Muslim foreign residents from India, the Philippines, and Europe who practice Hinduism or Christianity make up the remaining 5 percent of the population.

In April 2003, a seminar was held in Doha, Qatar, to build understanding between Muslims and Christians. Pictured here are the Muslim director of the seminar, Mohammed Jiham Al Kuwri (left), and the archbishop of Canterbury, the leader of the Church of England.

Islam

According to Islamic tradition, the Prophet Mohammad received revelations from God, or Allah, in the seventh century. These revelations were recorded in a holy book called the Qur'an (more commonly called the Koran in the West). They became the foundation of a new religion called Islam, which means "submission to God." Muslims believe that Mohammad is the last in a series of prophets that includes Abraham and Jesus. The five pillars of Islam describe the basic practices required of Muslims: professing that "there is no God but God and Mohammad is his messenger," praying five times daily, fasting during the holy month of Ramadan, giving alms (charity) to the poor, and making a pilgrimage to Mecca, the birthplace of Mohammad.

After Mohammad's death, his followers disagreed upon the method of choosing a successor and interpreting the Qur'an. The Sunnis believed that the community of faith should elect Mohammad's successor and that the Qur'an should be the final authority on all religious matters. According to the Shi'ites, only Mohammad's direct

Did You Know?

Five times a day, the call for prayer issues from loudspeakers in the mosques. Wherever they are, Muslims stop what they're doing, complete a cleansing ritual, then face the holy city of Mecca and pray. Offices and public buildings in Qatar have special areas set aside for the ritual cleansing and prayer. On Fridays, Islam's holy day, most men pray in the mosque.

WAHHABISM IN QATAR

The Wahhabi movement began in the mid-1700s, when Mohammad ibn Abd al-Wahhab began preaching that Sunni traditions must be reformed. He argued that the practices of venerating Muslim saints (honoring saints with shrines and ritual devotional acts), decorating mosques, and living lavishly were inconsistent with Islam. In an effort to establish his strict vision of Islam, Abd al-Wahhab called for *jihad,* or holy war, against anyone, Muslim or not, who disagreed with his beliefs. The Al Saud family of northeastern Arabia accepted the Wahhabi approach to Islam, and when Ibn Saud established the kingdom of Saudi Arabia in the early twentieth century, Wahhabi beliefs became the official form of Islam there.

The Al Thani, the Qatari royal family, also follow Wahhabi beliefs. As a result, Wahhabi beliefs and customs permeate Qatari society. Men and women are segregated in most areas of society, including schools, government offices, shops, and mosques. Some buildings even provide separate elevators for men and women. Muslim women are required to wear clothing that covers all but their face when they go out in public. Despite these restrictions, Wahhabism in Qatar is not as repressive as the form practiced in Saudi Arabia. For example, women are allowed to drive cars, non-Muslim women do not have to be covered in public, and alcohol is available in Qatar for non-Muslims.

descendants should be allowed to succeed him as the Islamic leader. Shi'ites believe that these leaders, known as *imams,* are divinely guided in their interpretation of the Qur'an. (To learn more about Islam, see pages ix–xii in the introduction to this volume.)

(For more information about Wahhabism, see pages 62–64 in this volume.)

Everyday Life

A typical Qatari family today enjoys a life that was unimaginable six decades ago, when a nomadic lifestyle was commonplace. The discovery of oil and natural gas and the subsequent income from these resources had a dramatic impact on life in Qatar, encouraging settlement in modern urban areas. Today, most Qataris live in cities and towns, and the government provides free health care, education, and housing assistance to its citizens.

Family Life

The Qatari culture is based on tribal identity. Groups of related families, called clans, form a tribe. The ties between members of a tribe remain strong today, even though most Qataris have exchanged nomadic lifestyles for modern, urban lives.

Qatari society is strictly segregated by gender. All public buildings—including mosques, government offices, and shops—have separate sections for men and women. Even separate elevators are provided in high-rises. Despite the segregation, women have more rights in Qatar than in neighboring Saudi Arabia, including the right to drive cars.

Marriages are still arranged, usually to solidify relationships within the tribe. Although the arrangements are often made when a girl is in her early teens, the wedding itself typically takes place after the bride's education is finished. Qatari wedding celebrations last several days, but the bride and groom rarely see each other since the men and women participate in separate ceremonies.

Dress

As Wahhabis, Qataris are bound by a strict interpretation of the Qur'anic guidelines for dress. Women are required to be covered when they appear in public. Although most wear Western-style clothing at home, outside the house they wear a long black dress called a *darraa* and a *hijab,* a black scarf or veil that covers their hair. Many women mask their faces as well, wearing a *battoulah* that leaves only the eyes, nose, and mouth visible. Girls begin wearing a veil in public as young as seven, adopting the *darraa* at adolescence. Non-Muslim women are not

Religious Qataris belong to the strict Wahhabi sect, which dictates that both men and women wear traditional dress in public. However, Western-style clothing is usually worn by children and non-Muslims.

required to cover themselves in public, although they are encouraged to dress modestly.

Qatari men wear a long white cotton robe called a *thawb* (THOHB) over loose pants. Like other Arabs, they also wear a headdress called a *ghutra* (GOH-trah). The black woolen cord that wraps around the *ghutra* is called an *agal*.

Education

Before oil was discovered, formal education was not available in Qatar. The only educational opportunities were offered by religious leaders, who provided a basic education for a small number of boys. In the early 1950s, oil income made the establishment of an educational system possible.

Today, the Qatari government provides a free, compulsory education for all its citizens, as well as for the children of foreigners who are employed by the government. Both boys and girls attend primary school for six years, intermediate school for three years, and secondary school for three years.

Prince Edward of England visits the Taimiyah secondary school in Qatar. In secondary school, Qatari students take specialized courses, such as business or teacher training, to prepare them for work.

Although the schools are segregated by gender, the same curriculum is offered to boys and girls through intermediate school. Students are encouraged to participate in specialized study programs at the secondary level. Male students may choose from technical, business, or religious courses, while female students may enroll in teacher training programs.

The school day typically runs from 7:00 A.M. until 1:00 P.M. All instruction is provided in Arabic, although English is introduced at the end of primary school and taught throughout the intermediate and secondary levels. The government covers all school expenses, including transportation to school, textbooks, uniforms, meals, and tuition.

Many private schools have been established to serve the foreign community. While they receive some financial aid from the Qatari government, they charge tuition to cover the rest of their costs. These schools usually provide instruction in the students' native language.

The University of Qatar, established in the 1970s, accepts both men and women, but the two groups attend separate sections of the university. Today, more women than men attend the university, although one reason for this is that families are more likely to allow their sons to attend foreign universities.

Recreation and Leisure

Sports are very popular in Qatar. Soccer—known as football in Qatar—is often considered the national sport. In Doha, fourteen stadiums are set aside for soccer games. Tennis, golf, and squash attract many athletes as well, and international tournaments bring in top players from

A DESERT TRADITION

Falconry, the sport of hunting with a trained bird of prey, is very popular in the Arabian Peninsula. Many men, especially those from wealthy families, train falcons to hunt bustards and other desert birds. During hunts, the falcon tracks down its prey, often covering 3 miles (5 kilometers) before the chase ends. Many falconers follow the hunt from horseback or in a jeep.

A man trains his hunting falcon in the Qatar desert.

around the world. Sailing is a favorite pastime, as are horse races and other equestrian events.

Camel races in Qatar draw large crowds. While there are several racetracks in the country, the most important one is near Dukhan. At times, more than 250 camels race over the 11-mile (18-kilometer) track. Spectators often follow them across the desert in four-wheel-drive vehicles, urging on their favorite jockey and camel.

Food

Qatari cuisine reflects the country's nomadic past as well as its Persian Gulf location. The nomads, who herded sheep and camels, prepared foods from ingredients that were easily carried from place to place. As a result, rice, dates, and lamb are staples in the Qatari diet. Qatar's location near prominent Persian Gulf trading routes introduced a variety of spices into the region, including those common to India and China. Foreign residents also brought with them new foods and styles of cooking that have been incorporated into the Qatari cuisine.

KABSA (CHICKEN AND RICE SKILLET)

1/4 cup butter or margarine
1 (2-1/2 to 3 pound) chicken, cut up
1 large onion, chopped
5 garlic cloves, minced
1/4 cup tomato sauce or puree
2 medium tomatoes, chopped
2 medium carrots, grated
Zest from 1 orange
3 whole cloves
2 cardamom pods (or 1/2 teaspoon
   ground cardamom)
1 cinnamon stick
Salt and freshly ground pepper
   to taste
3 cups chicken broth
1 cup long-grain rice
1/4 cup raisins
1/4 cup sliced or slivered almonds,
   toasted

Melt butter or margarine in a large skillet. Add chicken pieces and sauté until browned. Remove from skillet and set aside. Add onion and garlic to skillet and sauté until tender. Stir in tomato sauce or puree. Simmer over low heat 1 minute, then add tomatoes, carrots, orange zest, cloves, cardamom, cinnamon stick, salt and pepper. Cook 1 minute. Add broth and chicken pieces to skillet. Bring to a boil, then reduce heat and simmer, covered, over low heat for 30 minutes. Add the rice to the skillet, making sure that it is stirred into the liquid. Cover and simmer 30 minutes longer or until rice is tender. Garnish with raisins and almonds. Makes 6 to 8 servings.

Source: Adapted from *Mideast & Mediterranean Cuisines* by Rose Dosti.

While lamb is the favorite meat in the Qatari diet, fish and seafood figure prominently as well. Yogurt, rice, and *burghul* (cracked wheat, also known as bulgur) are the basis for many dishes. Muslims, following the dietary restrictions outlined in the Qur'an, do not consume pork or alcohol.

Because of the heat, the Qatari day begins quite early. A light breakfast of olives, cheese, and yogurt is often served around 6:00 A.M., since family members generally have to be at work and school by 7:00. The family gathers back at home around 1:00 P.M. for lunch, the main meal of the day. Lunch begins with appetizers, followed by fish or lamb stew, vegetables, salads, bread, and fruit. Typical main dishes include *matchbous,* a spicy lamb dish served with rice, and *hareis,* a dish of cracked wheat and lamb. These are often eaten in the traditional way, using flat bread instead of silverware to scoop up bites of stew. Sweet desserts, such as bread puddings and cheesecakes, are served on special occasions. A light dinner, very similar to breakfast, is eaten late in the day.

Arab foods, such as *hummus* (a spread made of chickpeas and sesame seeds), *tabbouleh* (bulgur wheat seasoned with mint and parsley), and *shawarma* (shavings of grilled lamb or chicken rolled up in flat bread), are widely available. Restaurants serving food from other cuisines, including Thai, Indian, Pakistani, and Iranian, are common in Doha, as is American fast food.

A WELCOMING RITUAL

Qataris traditionally serve *qahwa,* or coffee, to welcome guests. This ritual takes place in both business and social settings. Qatari coffee, which is similar to Turkish coffee, is served in small cups without any sweetener or cream. The host pours a few drops of coffee in each person's cup, in order of the guests' social standing. Sweet, fresh dates are served with the coffee. While hosts will offer to fill guests' coffee cups any time they are empty, two cups are considered polite. Drinking just one cup of coffee or accepting more than three cups is very bad manners.

Qataris drink coffee both at home with guests and in coffee shops throughout the nation.

Holidays and Festivals

Because Qatar is an Islamic country, nearly all of its holidays are religious in nature. These holidays are celebrated according to the Islamic calendar, which is based on a lunar year. As a result, the dates for the festivals vary from year to year.

Ramadan, the ninth month of the Islamic year, is a time for Muslims to show their devotion to God. During Ramadan, Muslims fast between sunrise and sunset. Food, drink, and other activities, such as smoking, are prohibited during the day. This discipline encourages compassion for the less fortunate. In Islamic countries such as Qatar, non-Muslims are not required to fast during Ramadan, but they are forbidden to eat or drink anything in public places. At the end of each day, families gather for a special meal, called *iftar*, that breaks the fast.

One of the biggest celebrations of the year is Eid al-Fitr. This period of feasting and visiting occurs immediately following the end of Ramadan. During Eid al-Fitr, Qataris don new clothes and children receive gifts from relatives. In Doha, street carnivals and fireworks add to the fun. The feasting and festivities generally last three days, although the celebration may continue for up to ten days when the date falls in the middle of the week.

Eid al-Adha, the Feast of the Sacrifice, is the other major Islamic holiday in Qatar. This celebration occurs during the *hajj*, the time when devout Muslims make a pilgrimage to the holy city of Mecca. It commemorates the willingness of Abraham to obey God's command to sacrifice his son. Because of Abraham's obedience, God allowed him to sacrifice a lamb in place of the child. In preparation for Eid al-Adha, families who are financially able purchase a sheep to sacrifice for a feast. One-third of the meat is given to the poor, one-third is shared with relatives, and the family prepares the remaining third for the feast.

Since most Qataris belong to the Wahhabi sect of Islam, few celebrate Mohammad's birthday, since the Prophet's birthday was not celebrated by early Muslims.

The only nonreligious holiday celebrated by Qataris is National Day on September 3, commemorating the establishment of an independent Qatar.

Qatar's Bedouin history is reflected in its rich cultural heritage, but Qataris also appreciate other cultures. This member of a German dance troupe was photographed in Doha in March 2003 during a carnival parade that featured cultural groups from all over the world.

The Arts

The *Bedouin* culture that lies at the heart of Qatar's society has influenced its arts as well as its traditions of hospitality and family ties. From crafts such as jewelry making to dance and music, the influence of the nomadic past is seen in the Qatari arts of today.

Traditional Crafts

For centuries, Qatari craftspeople have been known for their gold jewelry, embroidery, and weaving. Gold jewelry, available in traditional marketplaces called *souks,* is made in both traditional and contemporary styles. Intricate embroidery using gold and silver thread decorates clothes made for special occasions. The Bedouin art of *sadew,* or weaving, continues today. Goat, sheep, and camel hair are all used to produce carpets, coverlets, and bags in bright colors.

Today, Qatar's Family Development Center, a program of the Qatar Foundation for Education, Science, and Community, provides training for women in the production and marketing of traditional arts and crafts. These items are often sold in the traditional souks in Doha and other cities.

Performing Arts

Poetry, storytelling, singing, and dance played an important role in nomadic life centuries ago, just as they do in Qatari culture today. Weddings and other family celebrations feature performances of traditional music, dance, and stories. Stringed instruments, such as the *rebaba* and *oud,* are among the most common traditional musical instruments. The Arab flute is also featured in many songs.

QATARI JEWELRY

For centuries, Qatari goldsmiths have produced some of the region's finest gold jewelry. Traditionally, jewelry is given to women upon their marriage. This jewelry belongs to them and is considered a safeguard against future catastrophes. If the marriage ends in divorce, the jewelry can be sold and the income used for living expenses.

Three items of jewelry are typically worn by Qatari women. The *mirtaesha* is a necklace that often covers the chest from neck to waist. Gold bracelets known as *kaff* extend over the hands, while the *tasa* is worn on the head.

The oud *is a traditional stringed instrument that is played in Qatar and other Arab nations with a nomadic Bedouin heritage.*

One favorite dance, the *ayyalah,* re-creates a battle scene. Dancers wielding sticks or swords pretend to fight each other as drummers beat out a rhythm on an assortment of percussion instruments. Traditionally, a big drum called *al-ras* is accompanied by three smaller drums, tambourines, and cymbals. As the dance progresses, each side challenges the other in song.

Saudi Arabia

The birthplace of Islam, Saudi Arabia is one of the richest countries in the world due to the immense reserves of oil and natural gas that lie beneath its surface and in the Persian Gulf. This desert kingdom covers much of the Arabian Peninsula, making it the largest country in the Middle East. It was established as the result of an alliance between Wahhabi religious leaders and the Al Saud family, giving the royal family religious as well as political authority. The Wahhabis, known for their strict interpretation of Islam and insistence that theirs is the only true view of Islam, still control Saudi society today. Evidence linking some Wahhabi groups with international terrorism has strained diplomatic relationships with many Western countries, including the United States.

The Saudis

An estimated 24 million people live in Saudi Arabia, nearly one-fourth of them citizens of another country. The Saudi population is quite young, with about half under the age of fifteen. This trend is expected to continue because Saudi Arabia has one of the fastest-growing populations in the world.

Most of the citizens of Saudi Arabia share a common Arab heritage. About two-thirds are descendants of the tribes that have lived in Arabia since ancient times. Others have ancestors who made religious

FAST FACTS

✔ **Official name:** Kingdom of Saudi Arabia

✔ **Capital:** Riyadh

✔ **Location:** Arabian Peninsula, north of Yemen

✔ **Area:** 756,985 square miles (1,960,582 square kilometers)

✔ **Population:** 24,293,844 (July 2002 estimate)

✔ **Age distribution:**
0–14 years: 42%
15–64 years: 55%
over 65 years: 3%

✔ **Life expectancy:**
Males: 67 years
Females: 71 years

✔ **Ethnic groups:** Arab 84%, Indian and Pakistani 10%, African (excluding Egyptian Arabs) 1%, Filipino 1%, other 4%

✔ **Religions:** Muslim 100%

✔ **Languages:** Arabic

✔ **Currency:**
Saudi riyal (SAR)
US$1 = 3.75 SAR (2003)

✔ **Average annual income:** US$8,460

✔ **Major exports:** Oil, gas, cereals

Source: CIA, *The World Factbook 2002;* BBC News Country Profiles; www.worldstatesman.com

pilgrimages to Mecca from other parts of the world and decided to stay in the Hejaz, making that region the most culturally diverse in Saudi Arabia.

For centuries, there were two main traditions in Saudi Arabia—the nomadic lifestyle of the *Bedouins* and the settlements of farmers and merchants. Although the Bedouins traveled over wide areas as they moved their herds of camels and goats between grazing grounds, they kept to themselves and had little interaction with outsiders. In contrast, people in the Hejaz came in contact with the wide range of cultures and ideas of pilgrims coming to Mecca as well as traders following the caravan trade routes that stretched from southern Arabia to the Mediterranean. Today, the Hejaz has several communities of Indians, Indonesians, Persians, and Africans.

Before the middle of the twentieth century, tribal and family affiliation determined an individual's social standing. Today, as the

> ### Did You Know?
> Although Saudi Arabia is the largest country in the Middle East, it has a relatively small population. In comparison, Egypt, which is about half the size of Saudi Arabia, has almost three times as many people.

These Saudi workers are taking a break. So many foreigners have poured into wealthy Saudi Arabia seeking jobs that the government, to ensure that there are enough jobs for its own citizens, is working to reduce the number of foreigners in Saudi Arabia.

nomadic lifestyle is dying out and modern technology is creeping into everyday life, educational achievements and economic level are more likely to determine people's standing in Saudi society.

Saudi Arabia, like many other oil-rich nations in the Middle East, has a large number of foreign residents who have come seeking work. In 2003, over 5 million foreigners lived in Saudi Arabia. Most are from other Arabic-speaking nations, including Egypt, Yemen, Jordan, Syria, and Kuwait. There is also a large number of Asian residents, from Pakistan, India, the Philippines, Sri Lanka, and South Korea. Other foreign nationals are from Africa, Europe, and North America. Saudi Arabia, faced with a rising unemployment rate for its own citizens, is working to reduce the number of foreigners employed and living in the country.

Land and Resources

Saudi Arabia, the largest country in the Middle East, is about one-fifth the size of the United States. It covers most of the Arabian Peninsula, the landmass that lies between the Red Sea and the Persian Gulf. Jordan, Iraq, and Kuwait border Saudi Arabia on the north. Qatar and the United Arab Emirates share small sections of Saudi Arabia's eastern border, and Yemen and Oman lie to the south.

ANCIENT HISTORY

Geologists believe that the earth's landmasses sit upon plates—slabs of solid rock—that are in constant motion. The molten center of the earth exerts pressure upon the plates, shifting them over time. The edges of these plates are often the site of mountains, earthquakes, and volcanic activity. In addition, cracks often appear in weak areas near the edges of plates.

The Arabian Peninsula formed because of such cracks. One crack occurred in the present-day Persian Gulf, separating the peninsula from the rest of the Eurasian Plate. In the west, a crack developed along the edge of the African Plate. This crack, or fault line, is known today as the Great Rift Valley. It extends more than 3,000 miles (4,828 kilometers), from Syria to Mozambique. The Jordan River Valley, the Dead Sea, the Gulf of Aqaba, and the Red Sea all formed within the Great Rift Valley.

As the plates shifted along the Great Rift Valley fault line, the western edge of the Arabian Peninsula was pushed upward, forming the mountains in the Hejaz and Asir regions. In the east, the edge of the plateau dropped below the waters of the Persian Gulf. The plants and animals that had been living there died, creating sedimentary layers that would later become some of the richest oil deposits in the world.

Geography

Saudi Arabia lies on a plateau that juts out of the Red Sea in the west, slanting down as it moves eastward to the Persian Gulf. There are five major regions within Saudi Arabia: the western mountains, the central plateau, the deserts, northern Arabia, and the eastern lowlands.

Western Mountains

Mountains mark the western edge of Saudi Arabia, from Yemen northward to Jordan. In most places, these mountains are part of an unbroken ridge that has few natural harbors or coastal plains. The northern mountains are known as the Hejaz (he-JAZ) and the southern mountains as the Asir (a-SEER).

The Hejaz extends from Jordan in the north to the port of Jeddah (JIH-duh) in the south. Mecca and Medina, the two holiest cities in Islam, are located within the Hejaz. The mountain ridge of the Hejaz, which means "barrier" in Arabic, averages 5,000 feet (1,500 meters) in

A building near Najran, in the southwestern corner of Saudi Arabia, is pictured with the mountains of Asir in the background. Asir, along with the mountainous region of Hejaz to the north, makes up Saudi Arabia's western boundary along the Red Sea.

elevation, although some summits reach over 8,000 feet (2,500 meters). The gentle eastern slopes of the ridge were shaped by lava flows millions of years ago. *Wadis*, riverbeds that are usually dry, are carved into the eastern slopes. They carry runoff from the infrequent rains to the plains, where the water soaks into the ground, replenishing underground water sources and creating *oases* (oh-AY-seez)—green, fertile areas surrounded by desert. The largest oasis city in the eastern Hejaz region is Medina.

One of the few gaps in the mountains of the Hejaz occurs near Jeddah. Historically, traders crossed this gap to reach the cities of Mecca and Medina in the interior of the peninsula, enabling the region to become one of the most important and prosperous on the peninsula in ancient times. Today, Mecca and Medina—the cities where Islam was established—draw millions of Muslim visitors each year.

The Asir region extends southward from the Hejaz. Here, the mountains are higher in elevation, reaching 9,000 to 12,000 feet (2,700

Muslims all over the world celebrate Ramadan. During this month-long observance, Muslims show their devotion to God. Here, thousands of Muslim pilgrims visit the Grand Mosque of Medina in Saudi Arabia at the beginning of the holy month.

to 3,700 meters). The only forest in the entire Arabian Peninsula is found in the Asir. A coastal plain known as the Tihamah lowlands also develops here, the site of ancient trade routes that linked prosperous southern Arabia with Mecca and Medina. Agriculture is a mainstay of the region, both in the mountain valleys of the western ridge and the oases that dot the gentle eastern slopes.

Central Plateau

The Najd (NEHJD), the central region of Saudi Arabia, lies just east of the Hejaz. Most of the Najd is covered by ancient volcanic rock, although there are also areas of sandy desert and mountains. The Jabal Tuwayq, a curved ridge in central Najd, is home to most of the oases in this region. Because towns and cities grew up around the oases, Jabal Tuwayq is the most heavily populated area in the Najd. Riyadh, the capital city, is located in Jabal Tuwayq.

The Great Deserts

Three large deserts—known as the Great Deserts—border the Najd on the north, east, and south. Together, they cover more than one-third of Saudi Arabia.

North of the Najd is An Nafud (an-na-FOOD), a region marked by huge, crescent-shaped sand dunes. Some of the dunes in An Nafud, whose name means "red desert" in Arabic, rise more than 300 feet (90 meters) high and extend several miles in length. These long dunes are separated by

DESERT DETAILS: THE RUB AL-KHALI

- The largest area of uninterrupted sand in the world, the Rub al-Khali covers one-fourth of Saudi Arabia's surface.
- The Empty Quarter is one of the driest places on earth. Sometimes, more than a decade passes without measurable rainfall.
- Sand dunes in the Rub al-Khali can stretch more than 25 miles (40 kilometers) long and reach nearly 1,000 feet (300 meters) high.
- The Rub al-Khali extends into the United Arab Emirates, Oman, and Yemen. Borders between Saudi Arabia and these countries are often undefined in the Empty Quarter.
- The world's largest oil field, al-Ghawar, is located in the Empty Quarter.
- The first European exploration of the Rub al-Khali didn't take place until the 1930s.
- Located within the ultra-arid Rub al-Khali is the Umm al-Samim—a dangerous expanse of quicksand, into which whole groups of travelers are said to have disappeared.

valleys up to 10 miles (16 kilometers) wide. Strangely shaped sandstone formations edge the desert, carved by frequent sandstorms. Reliable watering spots and the grasses that appear after infrequent rains have made An Nafud an important grazing site for Bedouin camel herds.

East of the Najd is the Ad Dahna, a narrow desert that stretches nearly 80 miles (125 kilometers) from north to south, connecting An Nafud and Rub al-Khali. Sometimes called the "river of sand," the dunes in the Ad Dahna share the same reddish color as the An Nafud, especially in the north. Although Bedouins use the Ad Dahna for winter grazing, water is more limited there than in An Nafud.

The southern tip of the Ad Dahna joins the Rub al-Khali (roob-al-KHAH-lee), the world's largest sand desert. Often called the Empty Quarter, the Rub al-Khali extends 750 miles (1,200 kilometers) across the southern part of Saudi Arabia and is about 450 miles wide (720 kilometers) at its widest point. The surface varies from ever-shifting

In 1999, Jamie Clarke, a Canadian explorer, pictured here with the camels that were his transportation, set out with a Bedouin guide and others to trek across the Rub al-Khali, a vast desert in southern Saudi Arabia.

sand dunes to flat sheets of sand. Little water is available and few plants grow here, making the Rub al-Khali unsuitable for grazing.

Northern Arabia

North of An Nafud, a plateau crisscrossed with wadis forms the northern region of Saudi Arabia known as Badiyat ash-Sham. Although a part of the Syrian Desert, it is covered with grasses and other vegetation. It is considered prime grazing land.

Eastern Lowlands

Eastern Arabia is often called Al-Hasa (ahl-HAH-suh), after the large oasis in the region by the same name, although it includes the entire strip of land east of the Ad Dahna desert. Starting near the edge of the Ad Dahna, the as-Summan Plateau—a barren, rocky region—extends eastward toward the Persian Gulf, gradually decreasing in elevation. The plateau ends at the coastal plain, a flat lowlands area that is mostly sand or gravel desert. Marshes and salt flats appear occasionally near the coastline.

Did You Know?

Al-Hasa is the largest and most fertile oasis in Saudi Arabia.

Major Cities

Although Saudi Arabia once had many nomadic tribes, about 90 percent of Saudis live in cities today. The most important criterion for a city in this hot, arid land is a dependable water supply. In recent decades, technology has enabled deep wells to be dug, tapping into Saudi Arabia's underground water sources. These wells have accelerated the growth of Saudi cities.

About one-third of all Saudis live in the urban area surrounding Riyadh, the capital city of Saudi Arabia. Another third live in the western mountains. In this region, Jeddah, Mecca, and Medina are the most populous cities. Ad Dammam, an oil port in eastern Saudi Arabia, and the surrounding area are home to the final third of the population.

Riyadh

The capital of Saudi Arabia, Riyadh is a large, modern city. High-rise office buildings and hotels surround the center of the city, which is known as Old Riyadh. At one time, the city was surrounded by a wall, but it was demolished in the 1950s as Riyadh began to grow. Just outside of Riyadh, traders meet every day to buy and sell camels at one of the largest markets of its kind in the Middle East.

Jeddah

The most important port on the Red Sea coast of Saudi Arabia, Jeddah was Saudi Arabia's most prosperous city until the discovery of oil changed the country's economy. Historically, Jeddah's location near the only gap through the western mountain ranges helped it grow into a major economic center. In addition to the caravan trade routes between southern Arabia and the Mediterranean, overseas trading ships often docked at Jeddah's ports. The vast majority of Muslims making their pilgrimage to Mecca travel through Jeddah. Today, Jeddah remains a bustling, prosperous city. Its traditional *souk,* or marketplace, draws many visitors, as do its modern business centers.

Mecca and Medina

The two holiest cities in Islam are located in Saudi Arabia—Mecca, birthplace of the Prophet Mohammad, and Medina, the first city to

PREPARING FOR THE PILGRIMS

All Muslims have a religious duty to complete a hajj during their lifetime if their health and their financial means allow them to do so. Over the past few decades, world events such as the fall of the Soviet Union and innovations that have made travel easier and cheaper have contributed to a dramatic increase in the number of Muslims making the annual pilgrimage. Today, over 2 million pilgrims arrive in Mecca in Dhu al-Hijja (the twelfth month of the Islamic calendar) each year to take part in the hajj ceremonies.

This influx of visitors from around the world creates an enormous logistical challenge for the Saudis. The millions of visitors must have transportation to Mecca, temporary tent housing, and food. Sanitation, first aid, and medical centers must be provided. Hundreds of thousands of sheep, cattle, and camels must be made available to pilgrims for the ritual sacrifice and donation of meat to the needy that is an integral part of the hajj. Many of the pilgrims, coming from around the world, don't speak Arabic.

In 2001, the Saudi government spent nearly $200 million to prepare for the hajj. Much of the money went to improve the temporary housing areas and *infrastructure* in an effort to prevent tragedies like the fire in 1997 and stampede in 1998 that together killed 462 pilgrims. The government has also had to limit the number of visas issued for the hajj. Although preparing for the pilgrims is a costly responsibility, the Saudis view it as their religious duty since they are the keepers of the holy city of Mecca.

convert to Islam. Over 2 million Muslims travel to Mecca each year during the *hajj* (pilgrimage) season. Their destination is the Grand Mosque at the center of Mecca, which houses the Ka'ba in its courtyard. (The Ka'ba is a black stone sanctuary that, according to Islamic tradition, was originally built by Adam, the first man, and later rebuilt by Abraham and his son Ishmael as a place to worship God. All

Muslims visiting Mecca, the birthplace of the Prophet Mohammad, walk in front of the Grand Mosque, or Haram, in 2003. More than 2 million Muslims visit this holy city during the hajj *season.*

Muslims face the Ka'ba when they pray.) During the hajj, all pilgrims wear white seamless gowns to show that everyone is equal before Allah. The week-long hajj celebration includes special ceremonies, prayers, and feasts. Non-Muslims are not allowed to enter Mecca or the holy sites in the vicinity at any time.

Medina is an oasis city to the north of Mecca. When Mohammad began preaching about Islam, he and his followers were persecuted in Mecca. They moved to Medina, where the city leaders agreed that everyone would convert to Islam if Mohammad would become their leader. Medina later became a center of Islamic study. Today, many Muslims visit Medina after the hajj.

Ad Dammam

Ad Dammam is located in eastern Saudi Arabia, just across the channel from the island of Bahrain. Originally three villages, al-Dammam, Dhahran, and al-Khobar today are one large urban area known as Ad Dammam. Less than a century ago, people in this area fished and dove for pearls to make a living. Today, the urban area is the center of a thriving industry built around oil. (One-fourth of the world's proven oil reserves are found in the oil fields around Ad Dammam.) Most of the water for this area comes from desalination plants, which convert seawater to drinking water.

Climate

With the exception of Asir in the southwest, Saudi Arabia has a desert climate. Less than 4 inches (10 centimeters) of rain fall annually in most areas, and this rainfall is sporadic. Typically, one or two showers occur each year, creating flash floods. It is not unusual, however, for the desert areas to go for years without rain. In contrast, Asir receives up to 20 inches (50 centimeters) of rain annually, most of it between October and March. The rains come as a result of Asir's location near the tropics and the monsoons (heavy rains) spawned by the Indian Ocean.

In the interior, blazing hot temperatures during the day are offset by cold nighttime temperatures during much of the year. Summer temperatures average 113° F (45° C) during the day, although they may reach as high as 129° F (54° C). Spring and fall are more comfortable, with highs closer to 84° F (29° C). Overnight lows in the winter rarely fall below freezing, but the constant wind creates a bitterly cold environment.

Along the east and west coasts, the temperature swings are smaller. Daily highs seldom top 100° F (38° C). High humidity—85 to 100 percent—can make these regions very uncomfortable, however. Severe sand and dust storms caused by the *shammal*, a northwesterly wind that blows during the summer months, often interrupt travel in eastern Arabia.

Natural Resources

Saudi Arabia's most important natural resources are its oil and natural gas fields. The country's oil reserves are the largest in the world, while the natural gas reserves rank fourth (behind Russia, Iran, and Qatar). Oil, discovered in the late 1930s, quickly transformed Saudi Arabia from one of the poorest to one of the richest countries in the world. In 2002, experts estimated that Saudi Arabia's oil fields held 1.8 billion barrels. (A barrel of petroleum contains forty-two gallons.)

While Saudi Arabia's oil and natural gas reserves provide great wealth, its aquifers (underground water sources) are integral to life

A fisherman makes his way along a sandbar near Ad Dammam, on the Persian Gulf. The site of the first discovery of oil in Saudi Arabia, in 1938, Ad Dammam is also one of the main oil-tanker ports in the nation. Saudi Arabia boasts the largest oil reserves in the world.

Did You Know?

The United States imports 1.5 million barrels of crude oil from Saudi Arabia each day.

and agriculture in the desert region. Water has been discovered far beneath the surface in many areas, and deep wells have been dug to access these water sources. In addition, desalination plants have been built on both coasts to provide additional water. (*Desalination* is a process by which saltwater is converted to water suitable for drinking and irrigation.)

Plants and Animals

Oases, which have enough water for irrigation, support many agricultural crops, including date palms and other fruit trees, grains, and vegetables. The mountains in Asir receive plentiful rainfall, making agriculture possible there as well. People living in this region are able to grow tropical crops, such as coffee, on the heavily terraced

Hunting with falcons is a popular sport in Saudi Arabia. These traders are displaying hunting falcons for sale at a market in Riyadh. Hunters train their falcons to catch bustards, which, like the falcons, are large birds of prey.

mountainsides. Outside of these areas, however, plant life is limited. With the exception of the Rub al-Khali, most desert areas have grasses that spring up following a rain as well as low-growing desert shrubs and trees, including acacias and tamarinds.

Saudi Arabia once had an abundance of wildlife, including ostriches, gazelles, leopards, and oryx (a type of antelope). Unfortunately, most of these large animals have been hunted until they are extinct or endangered in the wild. Smaller mammals, such as foxes, panthers, hyenas, hedgehogs, hares, and wolves can still be found. Though there are only ten species of birds native to Saudi Arabia, many birds migrate to the area in the winter. Flamingos and pelicans are often seen near the coasts and marshlands, while eagles, partridges, thrushes, and other birds are found in the south. Bustards—large game birds—are often hunted by falconers, who hunt using trained birds of prey. Over 100 species of lizards and 53 snake species—many of them poisonous—are found in Saudi Arabia.

Today, Saudi Arabia has several nature reserves dedicated to preserving and restoring the populations of its native animals. More reserves are planned for the future.

THE CAMEL SPIDER

There are many stories told about the camel spider—an arachnid that isn't really a spider, but rather a *solifugid*, a creature that has features of both spiders and scorpions. The stories describe a creature that is bigger than a human hand and that can jump more than five feet (1.5 meters) straight up in the air. Some say that the camel spiders are poisonous, so lethal that they can kill an adult camel with one bite. Others tell of camel spiders chasing people, even those in Humvees and other vehicles. They say that camel spiders quickly crawl up people's clothing until they reach the face. Then the camel spider attacks, with its sharp fangs and nerve-numbing saliva.

Like all urban legends, the stories told about the camel spider (also called a wind scorpion) have little basis in truth. Camel spiders—which are found in many regions throughout the world, including the southwestern United States—range in length from one to six inches (2.5 to 15 centimeters). They don't jump, but they are the fastest nonflying arthropods in the world, reaching speeds of up to 10 miles (16 kilometers) per hour. Camel spiders are nocturnal, coming out at night to hunt for insects, lizards, and scorpions. During the day, they burrow into the ground or rest in shadowed areas. Sometimes camel spiders appear to chase people, when in reality the creatures are scurrying to stay in the moving shadows. Although camel spiders tend to avoid humans, they will bite when cornered. But camel spiders are not poisonous. The main risk of injury to humans is shock or infection after the bite.

History

Ancient Days

Archaeologists estimate that people have been living on the Arabian Peninsula since the Stone Age. (*Stone Age* describes the time when people used tools and weapons made from stone. It began 2 million years ago and lasted until 4000 B.C.E. in some parts of the world.) Little is known about these early people.

By 4000 B.C.E., several advanced civilizations had been established in the region around the Arabian Peninsula. To the northeast, the Sumerian civilization flourished in Mesopotamia (present-day Iraq). The Dilmun civilization, known for its trading prowess, was established on the island of Bahrain and the coast of eastern Arabia. In present-day Pakistan and India, the Indus Valley civilizations flourished. West of Arabia, across the Red Sea, the foundations were being laid for the first Egyptian kingdoms.

> Southwestern Arabia was so prosperous that Roman invaders called it *Arabia Felix,* or "happy Arabia."

Saudis walk through the ruins of Dir'iyah, the first capital established by Saudi Arabia's royal family, the Al Saud. In 1744 the Al Saud, a powerful clan, joined forces with the Wahhabis to build a strict Islamic nation. Dir'iyah, near Riyadh, is a protected site that is being restored.

IMPORTANT EVENTS IN SAUDI ARABIA'S HISTORY

4000 B.C.E. The Dilmun civilization rises to prominence in eastern Arabia.

1000 B.C.E. Newly invented camel saddles enable the caravan trade to flourish.

4th century C.E. The Abyssinian Empire controls southwestern Arabia.

570 The Prophet Mohammad is born.

610 Mohammad receives revelations from Allah (God) and begins preaching about Islam.

632 Mohammad dies after gaining the loyalty of nearly all the Arabian tribes.

661 The capital of the expanding Islamic empire shifts northward to Damascus, Syria. Arabian importance dwindles.

mid-1700s Muhammad ibn Abd al-Wahhab begins preaching that those who do not follow his strict interpretation of Islam should be persecuted or killed. His followers become known as Wahhabis.

1932 Ibn Saud, leader of the Wahhabis, officially announces the Kingdom of Saudi Arabia.

1938 Standard Oil Company of California discovers oil in Saudi Arabia and establishes the Arabian American Oil Company (Aramco) to oversee operations.

1953 Ibn Saud dies. His son Saud ascends to the throne.

1961 Eleven oil-rich nations, including Saudi Arabia, announce the formation of the Organization of Petroleum Exporting Countries (OPEC).

1964 The royal family names Faisal as king, forcing Saud to give up the throne.

1973 The Saudis place an oil embargo against the United States and raise oil prices for American allies following the Yom Kippur War. Worldwide oil prices skyrocket, setting off a global recession.

1980 The Saudi government takes complete control of Aramco and its assets. Oil revenues decrease.

1982 Crown Prince Fahd ascends to the throne following the death of King Khalid.

1987 Iranian Shi'ites fight with Saudi security forces during the hajj. Over 400 people die.

1990 Iraq invades Kuwait and threatens Saudi Arabia. The Saudi government asks the United States for protection and allows U.S. troops to be based in Saudi Arabia.

1991 The Persian Gulf War begins when an international coalition attacks Iraq and forces it to withdraw from Kuwait.

1992 The Saudis experience a financial crisis following the Persian Gulf War. The Saudi government sends Osama bin Laden, an outspoken critic of the Saudi government, into exile.

1994 Saudi government revokes Osama bin Laden's citizenship.

1995 Crown Prince Abdullah acts as leader of Saudi Arabia due to King Fahd's poor health.

1996 Osama bin Laden establishes Al Qaeda—the Base—and urges Muslims to kill Americans.

2000 Suicide bombers attack the U.S.S. *Cole* in Yemen. Evidence shows that terrorists have ties to Al Qaeda and Osama bin Laden.

2001 Terrorists hijack planes and attack the World Trade Center in New York City and the Pentagon in Washington, D.C. Fifteen of the nineteen suspected hijackers were Saudi citizens; all had links to Al Qaeda.

2002 The Saudi government refuses to let U.S. troops use Saudi military bases for the war in Afghanistan.

2003 The U.S. military moves its bases from Saudi Arabia to Qatar after the Saudi government refuses to allow American forces to launch attacks on Iraq from Saudi Arabia.

From 4000 B.C.E. to about 1600 B.C.E., the Dilmun civilization was the most prosperous and important in Arabia. As it declined, the Minaean (mih-NEE-un) kingdom in Asir and southern Hejaz in southwestern Arabia gained power, with ample rainfall supporting agricultural development. The city of Karna (present-day Sadah, Yemen) served as the Minaean capital. The kingdom thrived from 1200 to 650 B.C.E., due to the trade route that developed between southern Yemen and the Mediterranean. As increasing numbers of trading caravans carried frankincense, myrrh, and spices north, the city of Mecca—a religious center for early Arabs who worshiped many *jinn,* or spirits—became an important trading center.

The Sabaean (sa-BEE-un) kingdom, located east of the Minaeans, rose to power about 750 B.C.E. and eventually gained control over most of the Minaean kingdom. Also known as Sheba, the kingdom was quite advanced technologically—a dam near the city of Marib provided water for agricultural irrigation. The Sabaeans continued to grow wealthy through trade, especially of frankincense.

In northern Arabia, the Nabataens (na-buh-TEE-uns) prospered by controlling trade routes from the southern tip of the peninsula to the Mediterranean region. By the fourth century B.C.E., they had established an independent state with strongholds in rocky areas, such as Madain Salih and Petra (in present-day Jordan). By 106 C.E., however, the Romans had conquered much of northern Arabia, making it a Roman province. Two centuries later, the Abyssinian (a-buh-SIH-nee-un) Empire in present-day Ethiopia gained control over southwestern Arabia.

In vivid contrast with southeastern Arabia, the harsh climate and limited water of the Arabian interior made it inhabitable for any length of time. As a result, most of the Bedouins living in the area were nomadic herders who moved from one grazing pasture to another. They traded with those who had settled in towns and villages near oases. While the people living on the coasts were exposed to many different cultures and beliefs through their trading relations with people from other countries, the Bedouins lived their lives relatively isolated from other regions.

The Introduction of Islam

The caravan trade that linked southern Arabia with the Mediterranean brought more than wealth to Arabia—it introduced new ideas. By the sixth century C.E., Jewish and Christian communities were firmly established in the peninsula. Many Arabs continued to worship jinn, following ancient rituals that included pilgrimages to religious cities. The city of Mecca, controlled largely by the Quraysh tribe, was the main center for jinn worship; the Ka'ba was a sanctuary for over 300 spirits.

Early in the seventh century, Abu al-Qasim Mohammad ibn Abd Allah ibn Abd al-Muttalib ibn Hashim—later known as the Prophet

In this illustration from the 1800s, Mohammad explains Islam to followers in Medina. Mohammad went to Medina (known then as Yathrib) in 622 to become its leader after encountering violence in Mecca. By the time of Mohammad's death in 632, nearly the entire Arabian Peninsula had proclaimed loyalty to him.

Mohammad—began preaching a new religion called Islam, which means "submission to Allah (God)." According to tradition, Mohammad began meditating in the mountains outside of Mecca at age forty. During one retreat, the archangel Gabriel appeared before him and revealed the word of God. In 610, Mohammad, began

The remains of the Prophet Mohammad are entombed in the Mosque of the Prophet in Medina, Saudi Arabia. The tomb's doors are pictured here. Mohammad, who was born in the city of Mecca around 570, made Medina his home in 622.

preaching about the revelations, the most important of which was that there was only one God.

Mohammad's teachings threatened the financial prosperity of many in the Quraysh tribe since he taught that jinn worship must end. After trying to reason with Mohammad, city leaders later resorted to violence against his followers in an effort to convince Mohammad to stop his preaching. In 622, people from the nearby city of Yathrib (present-day Medina) asked Mohammad to serve as their leader. He agreed, with the stipulation that everyone in the city would convert to Islam. In Medina, Mohammad established himself as both spiritual and political leader, leading armies in battle against unbelievers.

In 630, Mohammad's army gained control of Mecca, rededicating the Ka'ba as a center of worship for Allah. By the time of his death two years later, nearly all of the tribes on the Arabian Peninsula had proclaimed loyalty to Mohammad, although not all Arabs had converted to Islam. (Those who worshiped jinn were forced to convert. Christians and Jews continued practicing their own religions, although they had to pay a special tax.)

> **Did You Know?**
> The flight of Mohammad and his followers to Medina is today known as the *Hijra*. It marks the beginning of the Islamic calendar. Islamic years are counted from the year of the Hijra and marked as A.H. (Anno Hegirae, or year of the Hijra). The year 2004 on the Gregorian calendar converts to A.H. 1424–1425.

Following Mohammad's death, a series of leaders known as *caliphs* was chosen to rule over the Islamic world. In the early years, the caliphs acted as both spiritual and political leaders, but later their power was primarily political. The first three caliphs ruled from Medina. Under their leadership, the tribes of the Arabian Peninsula were united, and the Islamic empire expanded to include lands from present-day Spain to Pakistan as well as parts of northern Africa. By 661, control of the Islamic empire had shifted to Damascus (in present-day Syria), and Arabian importance in the Islamic world had begun to decline.

The Medieval Period

During the medieval period (700–1500), Arabia ceased to be the center of the Islamic empire. Caliphs ruled from Iraq and Syria, and later from Egypt, India, and Turkey. As the center of power in the Islamic world shifted further away from Arabia, the Najd became more and more isolated. Mecca continued to be important, since all

Muslims were expected to make a pilgrimage there at least once in their lifetimes. Medina became known as a literary and intellectual center, and one of the four schools of Islamic law was developed there.

By the fourteenth century, most Muslims making their pilgrimage to Mecca chose to travel through the Hejaz region, avoiding the deserts and mountains surrounding the Najd. As a result, the people of the Hejaz came into contact with many foreigners and a broad range of ideas, while the tribes of the Najd maintained their traditional Bedouin culture, often viewing outsiders with suspicion.

The Rise of Wahhabism

As Islam was established across more cultures, the way people practiced the religion began to vary, as did some of their beliefs. For instance, one group of Muslims believed that only Mohammad's direct descendants should be chosen as caliphs. After Mohammad's death, this group became known as the Shiat Ali, or party of Ali. (Ali was Mohammad's son-in-law and cousin.) The Shi'a (SHE-uh), as they became known, were loyal to the *imams*—direct male descendants of Ali—whom they believed to be infallible religious authorities. The Shi'ites (SHE-ites) made pilgrimages to the shrines of the imams and commemorated the martyrdom of Ali's son Hussein in a religious observance known as Ashura. Although some Shi'ite Muslims lived in Arabia, the majority were located in Iran and Iraq.

Arab tribes who had been forced to convert from their pagan religions to Islam also began incorporating some of their earlier religious practices into their version of Islam. They believed that natural objects such as rocks and trees had supernatural powers. Some of these objects became shrines for many Arabs.

In the mid-eighteenth century, a Muslim scholar from the Najd named Muhammad ibn Abd al-Wahhab began preaching against the Shi'ites and the resurgence of pagan beliefs. He reminded people that the Muslim holy book, the Qur'an (more commonly called the Koran in the West), says that there is only one God—Allah—who does not share his power with any persons or objects. His followers

Did You Know?

There are several different Shi'a sects, created when disputes occurred over which of Ali's descendants were the true spiritual leaders. The main sect, often called the "Twelvers" because of their belief in twelve imams, believe that the twelfth imam has been in hiding since 874 and will return as the "rightly guided leader." Another group—the Ismailis, or "Seveners"—revere the first six imams that the Twelvers claim, but support a different descendant for the seventh imam. The Ismaili imams have all been direct descendants of Ali.

became known as Wahhabis (wuh-HAH-beez) and his interpretation of Islam as *Wahhabism* (wah-HAH-bih-zum). As the movement grew, Muhammad ibn Abd al-Wahhab's message became more focused on the necessity of strict obedience to Islamic principles and law.

In 1744, Muhammad ibn Abd al-Wahhab agreed to work with Muhammad ibn Saud—a leader of the Al Saud, a powerful clan in central Najd—to create a country based on Islamic principles. Muhammad ibn Saud led his armies across the Najd to destroy shrines that the Wahhabis had identified as sacrilegious (something that violates a sacred principle). Within twenty years, most of the Najd was under the control of the ibn Saud and Abd al-Wahhab.

> The Al Saud is sometimes referred to as "the House of Saud."

In 1765, Muhammad ibn Saud died and his son, Abd al-Aziz, continued the fight. By 1803, the Wahhabis had destroyed the Karbala, the major Shi'ite shrine in present-day Iraq, and gained control of the Hejaz, including Mecca and Medina. Other powers in the Islamic world viewed the Wahhabi movement with trepidation, since most Muslims didn't follow such a strict version of Islam. In 1816, the Ottoman Empire, which had controlled the Hejaz, authorized an Egyptian army to push the Wahhabis out of Mecca and Medina. After taking control of those two cities, the Egyptians followed the Wahhabis to the Najd. Within two years, the Al Saud and the Wahhabis were defeated. The Egyptians forced most members of the Al Saud into exile, but the leader at the time—Abd Allah ibn Saud ibn Abd al-Aziz—was executed.

The Egyptians did not hold the Najd for long. The Al Saud, considered religious as well as political leaders, forced the Egyptians out of the Najd and much of the surrounding area by 1824. The Ottomans and Egyptians continued to hold the Hejaz throughout the nineteenth century, however. Eventually, the Al Saud and the Ottomans reached an agreement: the Ottomans would recognize the Al Saud's authority in central Arabia as long as the Al Saud continued to pay tribute to the Ottoman Empire.

Fighting within the Al Saud clan in the late nineteenth century weakened its political structure and contributed to a decline in its importance. In 1890, a rival clan led by Muhammad ibn Rashid succeeded in gaining control of Riyadh. The Al Saud fled eastward, seeking refuge in Kuwait.

The Rise of the Al Saud

One of the members of the Al Saud who was exiled in Kuwait was Abd al-Aziz bin Abd al-Rahman Al Saud, also known as Ibn Saud. Although young, he gathered a force and began to lead raids against the Rashidi clan. In 1905, when Ibn Saud took control of Riyadh, the Wahhabi religious leaders supported him as imam.

Early in the twentieth century, the Bedouin tribes of the Najd began adopting Wahhabism. As the Ikhwan, or brotherhood, movement spread, the Bedouins gave up their nomadic lifestyle and moved to agricultural settlements. There they strictly enforced a fundamentalist version of Islam—public prayers; separation of men and women; a prohibition against any innovations that had been added since the Prophet's lifetime; and a ban on music, smoking, and alcohol. Attacks were launched against any group that did not follow Wahhabi guidelines.

By 1915, tens of thousands of Ikhwan had joined Ibn Saud's campaign to establish a state based on Wahhabism. Soon Ibn Saud controlled the Najd and much of the territory to the north and south. Constrained by a British presence in southeastern Arabia, Transjordan, and Palestine, Ibn Saud bided his time. When the Sharif family, which controlled Mecca and the Hejaz under the authority of the Ottoman Empire, began to weaken in 1924, Ibn Saud led his army westward and conquered the Hejaz with little effort.

Building a Nation

As ruler over the newly expanded state, Ibn Saud had to work with many different factions, including the Wahhabis, the wider Muslim world, and Western leaders. The Ikhwan, determined to spread Wahhabism, often attacked opposing groups both within Arabia and across its borders in defiance of Ibn Saud's orders. Finally, in 1929, Ibn Saud defeated the Ikhwan in battle. In 1932, Ibn Saud announced the official formation of the Kingdom of Saudi Arabia, which included most of the Arabian Peninsula.

As Ibn Saud established his new kingdom, he sought to forge ties with former enemies and to strengthen ties with the tribes he ruled. Ibn Saud met regularly with tribal leaders and the *ulama* (religious leaders) to build consensus for his policies. Although he ruled over a poor kingdom that was hit hard by the global recession of the 1920s and

Ibn Saud (seated) began his rule as imam in 1905. Over the years he built the Kingdom of Saudi Arabia, whose formation was officially announced in 1932. Ibn Saud ruled as king until his death in 1953, when one of his sons, Crown Prince Saud (standing), took over.

1930s, Ibn Saud granted favors whenever he could, strengthening the ties of loyalty between his government and tribal leaders.

Sudden Wealth

In the early 1930s, oil was discovered in the Persian Gulf region. American and British oil companies quickly began competing for the rights to drill and produce any oil that might be found in the nations nearby. In 1938, Standard Oil Company of California won the right to explore for oil in Saudi Arabia and founded the Arabian American Oil Company (Aramco) to oversee operations. Aramco quickly found productive sites. With little modern infrastructure or technology in place, Aramco had to develop ports, find water supplies, and build offices, housing, and medical centers for its workers in addition to exploring for and producing oil. The company also assisted in developing agricultural sites.

Ibn Saud strengthened Saudi Arabia's ties with the United States and Britain during World War II (1939–1945) when he allowed the United States to establish an air base near Dhahran in eastern Arabia. Although the Saudis were officially neutral during most of the war, they did declare war against Germany and Japan in March 1945. After the war, Saudi Arabia joined the newly established United Nations (UN) as well as the Arab League, an organization of Arab-speaking states.

By the 1950s, ever increasing oil revenues were beginning to change the Saudi way of life. Roads were built, connecting the isolated cities, and social services, including education and health care, were funded.

New Leadership

When Ibn Saud died in 1953, his son, Crown Prince Saud, became king. Two other sons, Faisal and Talal, challenged Saud's authority on several occasions. By 1958, King Saud had been stripped of much of his power due to mismanagement of the kingdom's resources. He briefly regained his legislative and executive powers in 1960, but was forced from the throne in 1964 when the ruling family named Faisal king.

When Faisal took the throne, the Organization of Petroleum Exporting Countries (OPEC) was four years old. (OPEC is a group of eleven oil-producing nations that meet regularly to set oil production goals in an effort to maintain stable oil prices.) Oil revenues began increasing steadily, and Faisal began directing some of the money to new social and economic projects. Airports were built and roads improved, power plants were built, and schools and medical centers were expanded.

Although Saudi Arabia maintained diplomatic ties with the United States throughout the Arab-Israeli conflicts in 1967 and 1973, an oil embargo (prohibition of sales) was put in place against the United States for its support of Israel. In addition, oil prices were sharply increased for American allies. The oil embargo of 1973 had far-reaching effects; oil prices skyrocketed to four times their previous level, setting off a worldwide recession. Saudi oil revenues jumped, and new economic plans were funded.

King Faisal (center) receives a gift from U.S. Secretary of State William P. Rogers (right) in May 1971. Despite Faisal's plea at this meeting for U.S. support in the ongoing Arab-Israeli conflict, the U.S. supported Israel. This resulted in an embargo that sent oil prices skyrocketing.

King Khalid

Faisal was assassinated in 1975. Although his half-brother, Khalid ibn Abd al-Aziz, was named king, Crown Prince Fahd held much of the actual power in government affairs due to Khalid's poor health.

In 1979, a group of Saudi dissidents seized control of the Grand Mosque in Mecca, charging that the royal family had been corrupted by its association with the West and was no longer fit to rule. Because of its designation as a holy city, Muslims are not allowed to carry weapons or shed blood in Mecca. The government had to get permission from the *ulama* to enter the Grand Mosque with weapons and end the standoff. By the end of the conflict, over 250 people had died.

The Islamic Revolution in Iran unexpectedly spilled over into Saudi Arabia when Shi'ite radicals rioted in the Eastern Province just a few weeks after the Grand Mosque seizure. Although many Shi'ites had found employment with Aramco, the vast majority had not benefited from social improvements and still lived in poverty. Education and health care were limited, and few had access to electricity or clean drinking water. The government quickly moved troops into the area to end the demonstrations. Several protesters were killed and hundreds arrested. Following this and subsequent Shi'ite demonstrations, the Saudi government implemented a plan to improve living conditions in al-Qatif and al-Hufuf, two major Shi'ite towns.

In 1980, six Arab nations—Bahrain, Kuwait, Oman, Qatar, Saudi Arabia, and the United Arab Emirates—announced the formation of the Gulf Cooperation Council. The purpose of the organization was to enhance the economy and security of member nations through cooperation.

Fahd became king of Saudi Arabia in 1982, following Khalid's death. Abdullah was named crown prince. Fahd faced many challenges early in his reign. Although the Saudi government had taken complete control of Aramco in 1980, oil revenues began to decrease due to a surplus of oil on the world market.

In 1987, over 400 people died in Mecca during a clash between Iranian Shi'ites and Saudi security forces during the hajj, resulting in tense relations between Saudi Arabia and Iran for nearly a decade.

The Persian Gulf War

In August 1990, Iraq invaded the small nation of Kuwait. International condemnation of the invasion was swift and was backed by most Arab nations. The UN gave Iraq a January 15 deadline for withdrawing its troops from Kuwait. When that date passed with no action from Iraq, an international coalition force attacked and pushed Iraq out of Kuwait in about six weeks.

Saudi Arabia was among the many countries that denounced Iraq's actions and provided troops for the coalition force. It also allowed U.S. and other allied countries to base troops in Saudi Arabia, both for launching attacks against Iraq and for protection from Iraq. Many Saudi religious leaders spoke out against their country's involvement in a war against an Arab neighbor, but their loudest complaint was the deployment of Western troops—largely non-Muslim—in the Islamic holy land. After the war ended, the Saudi government allowed American forces to remain in the country, which increased the

A ROYAL PROBLEM

After Ibn Saud unified much of the Arabian Peninsula to create the kingdom of Saudi Arabia, he had to work to maintain the loyalty of the far-flung tribes. One way he did this was to marry women from the different tribes. According to Ibn Saud's own records, he married and divorced over 282 women. (Islamic law allows a man to have up to four wives at a time, and provisions for divorce are included in the law.)

When Ibn Saud established his kingdom, he proclaimed that only his direct male descendants could succeed him as king. By the time he died in 1953, he had fifty-eight sons—all of whom were princes in line to rule the kingdom. Ibn Saud also had many daughters, but their births were not recorded so no exact number is available.

The king and crown prince are chosen by the consensus of the royal family. King Fahd, the current king, is only the fourth son to serve as king. There are still many sons in line for the throne, but they are aging. For example, Crown Prince Abdullah—who is next in line to be crowned after Fahd steps down or dies—is in his late seventies.

At a time when Saudi citizens have to adjust to a new lifestyle with less money, there is growing resentment of the royal family's extravagance. With thousands of members, all of whom are supported by the government, the family's expenses keep growing. Much of the money is spent on royal palaces. There are 300 palaces in the city of Jiddah alone.

Fahd and his brother, Abdullah (left), are pictured in 1981.

tensions between the royal family and the growing number of Islamic fundamentalists.

Financial problems plagued Saudi Arabia in the years following the Persian Gulf War (1991). The Saudis owed the United States $51 billion for costs related to the Persian Gulf War. Repaying the debt was difficult due to low oil prices at the time, and Saudi Arabia had to resort to deep cuts in social services and other government spending. It also had to ask for loans from international banks.

Saudi Arabia Today

King Fahd instituted several governmental reforms in the early 1990s, including the establishment of the Majlis al-Shura, or Consultative Council, which advises the king on important matters. Saudi society remains very traditional, however, with strict segregation of men and women and limited rights for women. International groups continue to criticize Saudi Arabia's human rights record, pointing out that prisoners are regularly abused. Because of Fahd's poor health, Crown Prince Abdullah has been the acting Saudi leader since 1995.

The chairman of the Majlis al-Shura, or Consultative Council, Sheikh Mohammed bin Jubair, is pictured in 1997 in the council's chambers. Although the council was portrayed as a step toward modernization of the Saudi government when it was formed in 1993, in reality it passes no laws and holds little power.

Although the Saudi and American governments continue to work with each other, the relationship has been strained in recent years by a series of terrorist attacks against the United States and its interests, including the bombing of the World Trade Center in 1993, the 1996 bombing near the U.S. military base in Saudi Arabia, the 1998 bombings of U.S. embassies in East Africa, the attack on the U.S.S. *Cole* in Yemen in 2000, and the 2001 attack on the World Trade Center and the Pentagon. Although only one of these attacks took place in Saudi Arabia, many of the terrorists involved in the strikes have ties to Saudi Arabia. About three-fourths of the hijackers involved in the September 11, 2001, attacks on the World Trade Center and the Pentagon were citizens of Saudi Arabia, and evidence has since come to light that some members of the Al Saud family have financed various groups that have been linked to terrorism.

Despite the crown prince's denouncement of the September 11 attacks, the United States was not allowed to use Saudi military bases to launch its broad war against terrorism in Afghanistan and Iraq. As a result, American forces are now based in neighboring Qatar.

Economy

Although it has been working to diversify its economy in recent decades, Saudi Arabia still depends upon oil revenues to fund about 75 percent of its budget. In an effort to support the growth of the private sector, the government has offered incentives such as interest-free loans and free utilities.

Business and Industry

Oil and natural gas industries continue to dominate Saudi Arabia's economy. Service industries, including education and health care, are generally funded by the government. Efforts to diversify the economy have helped establish the petrochemical and steel industries. Saudi Arabia's rapid population growth in recent decades has fueled a boom in the construction industry.

Millions of foreign workers are employed in the oil and service industries. In the mid-1990s, the government ordered the gradual phase-out of foreign workers, with a goal of having Saudi citizens make up at least 25 percent of employees in every business by 2001. To assist in meeting this goal, the government privatized its telecommunications and electricity companies in the late 1990s, opening new jobs for its citizens. By late 2001, employers in professional fields had met or exceeded the 25 percent goal. However, manufacturers, service industries, and other low-level employers continue to rely upon foreign workers. Many Saudi youth consider laborer or assembly-line production jobs beneath them. As a result, the percentage of Saudi employees in entry-level and blue-collar jobs remains low. Plant managers complain that most Saudis hired for low-level jobs leave within a few months or have higher absentee rates than foreign workers.

The rapidly growing population is placing additional strain on the Saudi government. In many cities, water and sewage systems are outdated and must be upgraded in order to meet demand. Roads and airports also are in need of maintenance and expansion.

LOOKING FOR WORK

Since the 1950s, when oil revenues began pouring into Saudi Arabia, most Saudi citizens have not had to worry about working for a living. Oil prices climbed higher and higher, reaching a peak in the 1970s. By the 1980s, young people were paid by the government to attend college. After graduation, they were placed on the government payroll, expected to work only a few hours a day.

Today, the children of the Saudis who came of age in the 1980s are coming to the realization that life in the oil-rich kingdom has changed. Since 1980, the per capita income in Saudi Arabia has dropped from $28,000 to $7,000. Two major factors are responsible: the Saudi population has doubled since the early 1980s, and oil prices have dropped. The decrease in revenues means there is less money to go around. Compounding the problem is the fact that major investments are needed in Saudi Arabia's infrastructure. Already, many cities experience water rationing in the summer and rolling blackouts when electricity is unavailable.

Young Saudi adults now have to take any available job in order to support their families. Unemployment has soared; in 2001, nearly 20 percent of Saudis were out of work. Each year, a half million Saudis enter the workforce to compete for roughly 50,000 new jobs. Employers often receive more than one hundred résumés for every professional job opening they advertise. More than once, fighting has erupted as hundreds of men wait to apply for a limited number of jobs.

Media and Communications

Modern inventions such as radio and television have often clashed with Wahhabi sanctions against innovation. Until Saudi religious leaders are convinced that new technology can be used to advance Islam, it isn't allowed. For example, in the 1920s, Ibn Saud had to convince the Wahhabi leaders that radio could be used to broadcast the Qur'an.

While most Saudis have access to radio and television today, the content that is broadcast is subject to strict government and religious censorship. Any programming that presents non-Wahhabi viewpoints or criticizes the government is not allowed. In recent years, as satellite television has become more widely available, the Saudi government has had greater difficulty censoring programs. Instead, it's resorted to labeling programs such as those broadcast by Al Jazeera (a Qatari news network that often criticizes the Saudi government) as "poisonous."

A Saudi man in Riyadh reads a local newspaper in 2003. All media in Saudi Arabia, including newspapers, television, and radio, are strictly censored to support Wahhabi views. Ideally, according to Wahhabism, technology of any kind would not be allowed at all, but such a prohibition is nearly impossible to enforce.

Religion and Beliefs

Saudi Arabia holds a special place in the hearts of Muslims. It is the birthplace of the Prophet Mohammad and home to the holy cities of Mecca and Medina, where Mohammad received his revelations from Allah and established Islam in the seventh century. There is no freedom of religion in Saudi Arabia; all citizens are required to follow Muslim traditions.

Muslims believe that Mohammad is the last prophet in a line of prophets that includes Abraham and Jesus. They worship one God, whom they call Allah, the same God that is worshiped by Jews and Christians. Devout Muslims observe the five pillars, or duties, of Islam: professing that "there is no God but God and Mohammad is his messenger," praying five times daily, fasting during the holy month of Ramadan, giving alms (charity) to the poor, and making a pilgrimage to Mecca, the birthplace of Mohammad. (To learn more about Islam, see pages ix–xii in the introduction to this volume.)

Wahhabism

In the centuries following the founding of Islam, groups of Muslims developed different beliefs. The largest group, called the Sunnis, believed that Mohammad's successors should be chosen by the religious community, while the Shi'ite minority believed that only descendants of Mohammad could be considered legitimate successors. Sects formed within each of these larger groups as well. In Saudi Arabia, the Wahhabis, a Sunni sect, have shaped the country's social and religious customs since the mid-eighteenth century.

Wahhabism was established in the eighteenth century when Muhammad ibn Abd al-Wahhab began to preach against Muslims whose religious practices included anything other than the traditions established by the Prophet Mohammad. Wahhabi followers harassed and punished those who didn't conform to their beliefs, especially the Shi'ites.

Following an alliance between the Al Saud and the Wahhabis, the Kingdom of Saudi Arabia was established as a religious state, guided by Islamic principles. The Qur'an is the national constitution, and the king is believed to be Allah's representative on earth. The legitimacy of the royal family rests upon the support of the Wahhabi leaders.

The *mutaween* (religious police) patrol Saudi cities and towns, enforcing the Wahhabi view of Islam. Women must wear *abayas* (long black cloaks) and veils in public. Men and women are strictly segregated. Products from the West that are deemed offensive, such as Barbie dolls, are banned by the *mutaween,* who confiscate the products and fine or arrest those who try to sell them. They punish business owners who remain open during daily prayers and chase people who are late for prayers.

Women in Saudi Arabia are greatly restricted by Wahhabi law. These women in Jiddah can get away with jogging in public because they are wearing their long black abayas. The mutaween, or religious police, harass people who are caught breaking their strict rules.

In the 1970s, Wahhabism gained strength in Saudi Arabia. The ultraconservative Wahhabis, sometimes known today as the New Wahhabis or neo-Wahhabis, began using Islam as a way to justify political activities, including terrorism. The most well known of the new Wahhabis is Osama bin Laden, the former Saudi citizen who is believed to have masterminded the terrorist attacks against the United States on September 11, 2001.

Everyday Life

The conservative practices of Wahhabism affect all aspects of daily life in Saudi Arabia. All businesses must shut down during daily prayers, a ruling that extends to business-related technology such as automated teller machines (ATMs). Strict segregation of the sexes is observed. The *mutaween* enforce these and other Wahhabi principles through punishment and arrest.

WOMEN IN SAUDI ARABIA

One of the most striking aspects of life in Saudi Arabia for most Westerners is the restricted role given to women. Women must be fully covered in black when appearing in public. They are not allowed to talk to men who are not relatives. Schools, banks, even restaurants, are segregated by gender. Women may not drive cars; in fact, they must ride in the back seat.

While women and girls are allowed to attend school, they must view lectures at the university level on closed-circuit television to avoid having male professors in the same room with female students. There are few employment opportunities for women outside the fields of education and medicine. Within these fields, they can provide services only for other females. Hospitals are the only place where men and women are allowed to work side by side.

There have been signs recently that attitudes toward women in Saudi Arabia are changing. Adelah bint Abdullah, daughter of the Saudi crown prince, has established a commission to promote women's rights in business. The governor of Jeddah has named both men and women to participate on a panel to discuss economic development. And women are increasingly opening their own businesses.

Hanada Hindi, the first Saudi woman to become an airplane pilot, training in 2003.

Family Life

Saudi families are generally large, with six or seven children. Traditionally, extended families lived together in large compounds with separate quarters for men and women. Today, with over 90 percent of Saudis living in urban areas, parents and children are more likely to live in their own homes. A daughter lives with her parents until she is married, then moves into her husband's home. Typically, one son stays with his parents in the family home, even after marriage. While most marriages are still arranged by the bride's and groom's parents, the prospective couple may have some say in the decision today.

The oldest man in the family is considered the head of the household, responsible for making all decisions that affect the family. In today's nuclear family, the father typically assumes this role within his own family. However, an older male relative may continue to make decisions affecting the extended family.

Until recently, few Saudi women entered the workforce. Instead they remained at home to take care of the household and children. While education for women is still not encouraged by Saudi society, more and more women are seeking advanced degrees and careers outside the home. Given Saudi Arabia's social restrictions, however, employment is often hard to find; in 2003, less than 5 percent of the Saudi workforce was female.

Dress

Modern Saudis wear clothing that is very similar to that of their ancestors. Men wear an ankle-length white robe known as a *thawb.* During the winter months, a *mishlah,* or cloak, is added. Men wear the traditional Arab headdress, which consists of three parts. First is the *tajia,* a small cap. The *ghutra,* a square cloth that is typically white in the summer and red and white checked in the winter, covers the *tajia.* The black cord that holds the *ghutra* in place is called an *agal* (ah-GAHL).

Women have a wide range of clothing choices within their own homes. Western-style clothes, including jeans and fitted tops, are popular among younger women. In public, however, women must wear a long black cloak called an *abaya* (ah-BY-ah), along with a head scarf and veil that cover everything but the eyes. The *mutaween* punish and sometimes arrest women for not dressing properly in public, even for indiscretions such as letting a strand of hair escape from under the veil.

Education

Until the middle of the twentieth century, there was no formal educational system in Saudi Arabia. The few Saudis who received an education—all male—attended religious schools. Today, the kingdom offers a free comprehensive education for all citizens. Attendance at schools is not required, however.

Saudi primary schools serve students age six through twelve. Most children today complete the primary level, but the enrollment drops at the intermediate and secondary levels, each of which lasts three years. At the secondary level, students may choose between programs in science or arts. Many students attend colleges and universities in Saudi Arabia. Others continue their education at schools that specialize in business, agriculture, teacher training, or technology. Although women are allowed to continue their education through the university level, most Saudis still believe that females do not need more than a basic education.

Recreation and Leisure

The strict Wahhabi rules that have shaped Saudi Arabian society influence its leisure activities as well. Socializing with the extended family and close friends is the most common pastime, especially for women. Families often enjoy picnics together, and camping trips to desert areas and national parks are seen as a way to connect with ancient traditions.

Men have more recreational opportunities available to them than do women. Traditional sports such as camel and horse racing have been popular for centuries. Today, the races take place at racetracks rather than across the desert, but they still draw large crowds. Hunting—either with saluki hounds or falcons—is another tradition that has continued for generations. Most of the men who enjoy these traditional sports are wealthy, as these hobbies tend to be quite expensive.

Since the 1960s, modern sports have grown in popularity. Soccer, or football as it is called in Saudi Arabia, is the most popular sport, although basketball is gaining in popularity. The Saudi government has implemented several programs encouraging greater participation in sports. Sports facilities have been built in major cities, and sports camps focus on archery, tennis, and golf as well as soccer and basketball.

In addition to these organized sports, many Saudi men enjoy swimming and diving in the Red Sea. The coral reefs there are considered among the world's most beautiful. Across the country in Riyadh, an ice skating rink draws many men and boys (women are prohibited), while some amusement parks are reserved for women and children only. Women who can afford to join female-only clubs in large cities have access to health clubs. While swimming pools are often available in the clubs, women are required to wear a one-piece swimsuit as well as knee-length shorts.

> ### Did You Know?
> Cinemas, theaters, bars, and dance clubs are banned in Saudi Arabia. Many Saudis go to nearby Bahrain to enjoy these forms of entertainment.

Food

Saudis have two distinct culinary traditions that have melded over the centuries. In the interior, nomadic tribes relied upon dates, rice, and milk for their meals. Although they had large herds of goats, sheep, and camels, the animals were rarely slaughtered for food. Meat was eaten

BRAISED LAMB IN GULF TOMATO SAUCE

This dish has its roots in both India and Saudi Arabia, a nod to the early influence of Asian traders in Arabia as well as the cultural diversity in the Hejaz.

1 onion, chopped
3 tablespoons olive oil
1 clove garlic, minced (optional)
1 pod cardamom
1 cinnamon stick
1/4 teaspoon cumin
1-1/2 pounds lamb, cubed
Salt
1 pound ripe tomatoes (can substitute 16 ounces canned tomatoes, with juices)
1 cup water
1/4 cup plain yogurt
Minced parsley for garnish

Sauté the onion in the olive oil over medium heat until soft and transparent. Add the garlic, if using, and cook for another minute. (Some cooks prefer not to use garlic, believing that it interferes with the sweet spice mixture in this dish.)

Stir the cardamom, cinnamon, and cumin into the oil to release the flavors. Cook for a minute or two.

Raise the heat to medium-high and add the lamb, sprinkling with salt. Sauté until browned on all sides. Reduce the heat to medium-low.

Puree the canned or fresh tomatoes in a food processor or blender until nearly smooth, and add to the meat. Stir in the water and yogurt. Taste and adjust the seasoning.

Cover and simmer about 2 hours, until the meat is tender. The tomato sauce will thicken. If you prefer a thinner sauce, add water.

Traditionally, this dish is served over white rice, but it also goes well with spaghetti. Garnish with parsley and serve.

Source: Adapted from *The Arabian Delights Cookbook* by Anne Marie Weiss-Armush.

only on special occasions. Milk from the animals was often made into cheese and yogurt. When the nomads traveled near oases, they traded for wheat, fruits, and vegetables. People living in the towns and villages of the Najd relied upon grains such as rice, millet, barley, and wheat, as well as fresh fruits and vegetables. Most meat dishes used lamb.

The people living on the east and west coasts were influenced by the foods and spices of India and Persia (present-day Iran). Spices introduced by traders centuries ago, such as cardamom, cinnamon, cumin, and coriander, are still used in Saudi cooking today. Lamb and chicken are commonly used in meat dishes, although beef has grown in popularity.

Meals are traditionally eaten on the floor on a large carpet. Saudis sit on cushions rather than chairs and eat using the fingers of their right hand. The main meal is typically served in the early afternoon, after family members return home from work and school. Appetizers such as *baba ghanoush* (BAH-buh-GAH-nooj)—a dip made from eggplant—are served at the beginning of the meal, followed by vegetables and main dishes that usually combine meat and rice. Flat bread is broken into pieces and used to scoop up bites of food. Buttermilk, *laban* (a drink made from yogurt), camel's milk, and cola are other favorite beverages in Saudi Arabia. Coffee and tea are also very popular and are served at the end of every meal.

There is very little conversation during a meal; socializing takes place before and after the meal is eaten. Guests are always offered the choicest pieces of food. To decline foods that are offered is considered very rude.

Holidays and Festivals

Under the Wahhabi view of Islam, only two religious holidays are celebrated—Eid al-Fitr and Eid al-Adha. Although some Saudis celebrate Mawlid (the birth of the Prophet), Laylat al-Isra (the ascension of the Prophet), and Muharram (Islamic New Year), these holidays are not approved by the clergy. National Day, which commemorates the unification of the Kingdom of Saudi Arabia, is observed on September 23.

Eid al-Fitr

Eid al-Fitr marks the end of Ramadan, the holy month of fasting and prayer. During Ramadan, all markets and restaurants are closed from sunrise to sunset. After evening prayers at sunset, families and friends gather to break the daylong fast with a meal called *iftar*. As the sun sets on the final day of Ramadan, Saudis celebrate their most joyous holiday. New clothes have been purchased for the occasion, and family members exchange presents. Family and friends gather for feasts on each of the three days of Eid al-Fitr.

Eid al-Adha

Eid al-Adha, the Feast of the Sacrifice, is a four-day celebration that commemorates Abraham's obedience to God. Because he was willing to sacrifice his son to God, Abraham was allowed to sacrifice a lamb instead. Eid al-Adha is held at the end of the hajj season. Families

As part of the Eid al-Adha celebration each year, Muslim pilgrims in their white attire throw pebbles, symbolically "stoning" a pillar that represents the devil. It is believed that the devil showed himself to Abraham in this very spot in Mena, near Mecca. This photograph was taken in 2003.

slaughter a lamb or goat during Eid al-Adha, preparing some of the meat for themselves and giving the rest to relatives and the poor in their community. While Eid al-Adha is an occasion for celebrating family ties and God's mercy, it is generally a quieter, less lively holiday than Eid al-Fitr.

The Arts

As in other Arab nations, the arts in Saudi Arabia developed within the constraints and guidelines of Islam. The Qur'an forbids the depiction of humans and animals. As a result, most visual artists employ calligraphy, the art of beautiful writing, to embellish their work. In this art form, phrases and quotations from the Qur'an decorate tiles and other surfaces. Other artists create highly stylized geometric or floral designs.

The Bedouins are known for their intricate silverwork. The jewelry often includes semiprecious stones such as turquoise, coral, and pearls. Some Bedouin designs are said to provide protection against evil, while others reflect the shape of the hand to represent the five pillars of Islam. Bedouin artists are also known for their skills in weaving and embroidery.

Most of the music heard in Saudi Arabia is traditional Arab music. Chants and other songs are accompanied by the *oud* (OOD), a lute; the *riqq,* a tambourine; and the *rebaba* (reh-BAH-buh), a one-stringed fiddle used by Bedouins. Music is prohibited during religious services.

While each region of the country has its own traditional dances, the *ardha* (AHR-dah) is considered the national dance of Saudi Arabia. It is often performed at feasts and other celebrations. In the *ardha,* a fast-paced dance that symbolizes courage, poets sing traditional songs while men jump over swords to the beat of drums.

The Qur'an is recognized as the predominant work of literature in Saudi Arabia. Storytelling and poetry are among the most highly valued Saudi arts, and the ability to speak eloquently is greatly admired.

Syria

yria, located on the eastern coast of the Mediterranean Sea and south of Turkey, has served for centuries as a crossroads that connects Europe, Asia, and Egypt. The trade routes that crisscrossed Syria brought both wealth and conquerors. Its people lived under foreign control for centuries, but finally gained their independence after World War II (1939–1945). Today, Syria stands at its own crossroads in history. Accused of supporting terrorism and harboring weapons of mass destruction, Syria must find a way to prove these charges false or face international condemnation.

The Syrians

On its face, Syrian society is relatively homogeneous, with 90 percent of its citizens sharing an Arab heritage. In reality, Syrians who share the same religious background have more in common than those who share the same ethnic background. Society is splintered further by differences in the economic level and cultural heritage of people within each religious *sect* (denomination or group). Traditional dress, etiquette guidelines, and religious rituals can vary widely among the people of a particular religious group.

FAST FACTS

✔ **Official name:** Syrian Arab Republic

✔ **Capital:** Damascus

✔ **Location:** Eastern coast of the Mediterranean Sea, north of Lebanon and south of Turkey

✔ **Area:** 71,500 square miles (185,180 square kilometers), including the Golan Heights region (500 square miles; 1,295 square kilometers), which is currently occupied by Israel

✔ **Population:** 17,585,540 (July 2002 estimate)

✔ **Age distribution:**
0–14 years: 39%
15–64 years: 58%
over 65 years: 3%

✔ **Life expectancy:**
Males: 68 years
Females: 71 years

✔ **Ethnic groups:** Arab 90%, Kurds, Armenians, and other 10%

✔ **Religions:** Sunni Muslim 74%, Alawite, Druze, and other Muslim sects 16%, Christian 10%, Jewish (less than 1%)

✔ **Languages:** Arabic, Kurdish, Armenian, Aramaic, Circassian, French, English

✔ **Currency:**
Syrian pound (SYP)
US$1 = 46.69 SYP (9/03)

✔ **Average annual income:** US$1,040

✔ **Major exports:** Oil, gas

Source: CIA, *The World Factbook 2002*; BBC News Country Profiles.

Because of Syria's history as an often conquered region, extended families developed extremely loyal ties among themselves. Even today, most Syrians' first loyalty lies with their family and religious group rather than their ethnic group or national government. This clannish mentality has made it very difficult for the Syrian government to initiate programs that require cooperation and trust between the different religious groups. To combat this difficulty, the government has tried to emphasize the Arab heritage that most Syrians have in common.

Arabic is Syria's official language, although many Syrians are native speakers of Kirmanji (Kurdish), Armenian, Turkish, and Syriac. Many Syrians who live in urban areas speak French or English in addition to their native language. There are three forms of Arabic: classical Arabic, the language of the Qur'an; modern standard Arabic, the literary form of the language; and the spoken Arabic dialect unique to each region. Syrians speak many different dialects, each distinctive enough to enable others to identify a speaker's birthplace or city of residence by his or her speech.

Arabs

Syrian Arabs share a common language—Arabic—but their ancestry is diverse. While some trace their family line back to the tribes that lived on the Arabian Peninsula, others are descendants of Aramaeans, Chaldeans, Canaanites, and Assyrians. Today, the term *Arab* refers more to a Syrian's native language than ancestry.

The majority of Syrian Arabs—90 percent—are Muslim. Most Arab Muslims belong to the mainstream Sunni sect, but Alawite Muslims form a sizable minority. (The Alawite sect is an offshoot of Shi'a Islam.) The remaining 10 percent of Syrian Arabs follow Christian, Druze, and other religious traditions. There is a small Jewish population as well.

Kurds

The Kurds are descendants of nomads whose ancient homeland, known as Kurdistan, spans parts of present-day Syria, Turkey, Iran, and Iraq. Today, Kurds make up an estimated 8 percent of the Syrian population. Few Kurds today maintain a nomadic lifestyle. They have settled primarily in towns and villages in northeastern Syria. There is also a large Kurdish population living in the foothills of the Taurus Mountains, north of Aleppo. A small number of Kurds live in a settlement called Hayy al-Akrad (Quarter of the Kurds) on the outskirts of Damascus.

Most Kurds are Sunni Muslims, although there are small numbers of Kurdish Christians and Alawites. Syrian Yazidis—a religious sect combining traditions from Judaism, Christianity, Islam, and other old beliefs—are sometimes considered to be Kurds because they speak Kirmanji, a Kurdish language. About 160,000 Kurds living in Syria today are officially considered foreigners because they cannot prove that they or their ancestors have lived in Syria since 1945. As a result, they are not allowed to attend state-run schools, own property, or hold government jobs.

Most Kurds are farmers who grow wheat, barley, cotton, and rice. Kurds living in cities generally find work as manual laborers, foremen, or supervisors, although some serve in the military. Most city dwellers have adopted the dress and customs of the community that they live in.

The Kurdish language—Kirmanji—is generally spoken only among family and friends. Teaching Kirmanji in school or publishing any materials in the Kurdish language is against the law in Syria. The government does not want to encourage nationalism among Kurds for fear that an independence movement might gain strength and cause problems for Syria.

Armenians

Most Armenians living in Syria are city dwellers. Some have lived in Syria for many generations, but most are more recent immigrants who fled genocide in Turkey after 1915. (*Genocide* is the systematic murder of a group of people based on race, politics, or culture.) As a group, most Armenians live in the Aleppo area in northwestern Syria. A small number live in Damascus in Hayy al-Arman (Quarter of the Armenians). Most Armenians work in skilled trades and crafts.

Armenians continue to practice Christianity in Syria. Most belong to the Armenian Orthodox Church, but the Armenian Catholic Church is also active.

The Armenian community has worked hard to maintain its ethnic and cultural identity in Syria. Schools and newspapers help keep Armenian customs and traditions alive. As the government pushes for a united Syrian identity, Armenians have continued to stress their separate history and identity. As a result, many feel they are not well represented by the government.

Others

A small portion of Syria's population consists of Turkomans, Circassians (sur-KA-shee-uns), Assyrians, and Jews. The Turkomans are a Turkish speaking people who came from central Asia. Most Turkomans dress in the Arab manner and speak Arabic, but a few still keep Turkic customs. They are Sunni Muslims, usually herders or farmers in the Aleppo area.

The Circassians immigrated to Syria from the Caucasus Mountain region in present-day Russia in the nineteenth century. The Circassians are organized by tribes and are generally farmers, raising crops and livestock. Blacksmithing and masonry are also common professions. Circassians have retained many of their customs as well as their native language.

The Assyrians settled in the Khabur River area in northeastern Syria in the early 1930s. Although most Assyrians are farmers, the poor quality of the land in the region has forced many of them to migrate to urban areas. Most Assyrians are Christians who speak Syriac, one of the

Christians are a small minority in Syria. Most Assyrians in the country, who are descendants of an ancient people, fall into this category. This Catholic priest stands at the altar of Saints Sergios and Bacchus Church in Maloula, Syria, one of the oldest churches in the world.

original languages spoken in Syria. As the Assyrian community assimilates into the larger Syrian society, Syriac is slowly dying out.

Jews make up the smallest ethnic group in Syria. At one time, the Jewish community was a vital, prosperous part of Syrian society. After the establishment of the state of Israel, Jews came under attack as possible traitors. As a result, most Jews left Syria to live in Israel. Only about 250 Jews remain in Syria today.

Land and Resources

Syria is located on the eastern Mediterranean Sea. Turkey borders Syria on the north, while Iraq, Jordan, and Israel lie to its east and south. Lebanon is tucked in between southwestern Syria and the

Syria's diverse geography includes a coastal plain, mountains, and deserts. This photograph of a lake in western Syria was taken in 1999, when the region was experiencing a severe drought. The Barada River, which supplies Damascus with water from the mountains, can barely be seen.

Mediterranean Sea. Syria covers about 71,500 square miles (185,180 square kilometers), making it slightly larger than North Dakota. Since 1967, Syria's Golan Heights territory—about 500 square miles (1,295 square kilometers)—has been occupied by Israel.

Geography

Moving from west to east, Syria's diverse geography includes coastal plains, mountains, a fertile plateau, and desert. The western coastal plains that border the Mediterranean are quite fertile. People living in this region farm year-round, relying upon the abundant rainfall to grow many types of fruits and vegetables.

Just east of the coastal plain is Syria's main mountain range, the Jabal an-Nusayriyah. This range is also known as Jabal al-Alawiyya since it was home to many Alawite Muslims in ancient times. The mountains, with an average height of 4,000 feet (1,220 meters), block much of the moisture from the Mediterranean. As a result, the western slopes can be cultivated, but the eastern slopes are dry and rocky, suitable only for raising sheep. Another mountain range, the Anti-Lebanon Mountains, forms the border between Lebanon and Syria in the southwest. Mount Hermon, Syria's highest point at 9,232 feet (2,814 meters), is located in the Anti-Lebanon range.

THE EXTRAORDINARY EUPHRATES

The Euphrates River is the most important river in western Asia, flowing from Turkey through Syria and Iraq before joining the Tigris River to form the Shatt al-Arab. Extending over 1,700 miles (2,700 kilometers), the Euphrates is the longest river in the region. Although it is nearly a mile wide in some places, the Euphrates is shallow with shifting sandbars, allowing only small boats to navigate its waters.

The land between the Euphrates and Tigris rivers (in present-day Iraq) was known in ancient times as Mesopotamia. Here, some of the world's earliest civilizations—Assyria, Babylonia, and Sumer—flourished. According to the Old Testament, the Euphrates was one of four rivers flowing from the Garden of Eden.

Most of the water flowing through the Euphrates comes from the annual snow melt in the Armenian Mountains of Turkey. People in Turkey, Syria, and Iraq depend upon the water for irrigation and for the generation of hydroelectricity. Conflicts often arise concerning water usage. Turkey's construction of several dams and hydroelectric generating stations since 1990 has resulted in a sharp decrease in the amount of water available to Syria and Iraq. Likewise, Syria's al-Thawrah Dam diverts water that once flowed into Iraq.

East of the Jabal an-Nusayriyah and the Anti-Lebanon Mountains lies a plateau that covers eastern Syria. Although all of eastern Syria is arid, the region just east of the mountain ranges supports agriculture due to the rivers, including the Barada River near Damascus and the Orontes River, which parallels the Jabal an-Nusayriyah, that carry runoff from the mountains.

The famed Euphrates (yoo-FRAY-teez) River, site of the Fertile Crescent that supported several ancient civilizations, runs through the northeastern plateau and provides water for farming. The al-Balikh River and the al-Khabur, which feed into the Euphrates, are both important sources of water for the region as well.

The fertile plateau gradually changes into the rocky Syrian Desert that covers southeastern Syria, stretching beyond the Syrian border into Iraq, Jordan, and northern Saudi Arabia. Although there is enough sand in the desert region to create dangerous sandstorms, huge boulders and rocks are the region's most distinctive features. Few people live in the desert region, although winter rains enable nomadic herders to use the desert as a winter grazing ground. Several low mountain ranges are located in the desert region. In ancient times, desert cities were built near the *oases* that once dotted the region, but many cities were abandoned when the oases dried up or came under attack by hostile tribes. Two major oasis cities that continue to flourish are Damascus and Palmyra (known as Tadmor in ancient times).

Major Cities

Syria's cities, most of which are located in the fertile plateau region and the coastal plain, are home to nearly half of the population. They are growing rapidly, with more and more people seeking economic opportunities in the cities each year.

Damascus

Damascus (duh-MAS-kus), the capital city, has a population of over 4 million people, making it the largest city in Syria. It is located in the Ghutah Oasis at the foot of the Anti-Lebanon Mountains in southwestern Syria. Damascus is one of the oldest cities in the world, dating back to about 6000 B.C.E. Today, as in the past, Damascus is an important city for trade between Iraq, Lebanon, and Jordan.

Many ancient buildings remain standing in the Old City of Damascus. One of the most famous is the Ummayad Mosque, built in 705 C.E. Next to the mosque is the Azm Palace, built for the governor of

In the Old City of Damascus, old homes with courtyards such as this one have been refurbished and turned into cafés. Traditional souks, or markets, are also found in the streets of the Old City, making it a bustling, lively place.

Damascus in the mid-1700s. Traditional Arab *souks,* or markets, are also found in the Old City. There merchants and craftspeople offer both traditional and modern goods, handcrafted jewelry, tailoring services, and foods for sale.

The modern sections of Damascus have wide streets, large apartment buildings, and tall office complexes. Not everyone likes the modern architecture, however. Many Syrians believe that the traditional buildings with low, thick walls were much cooler than the present-day high-rises that seem to trap the heat. The National Museum of Damascus, the University of Damascus, and the National Library are well-known landmarks in Damascus.

Aleppo

Aleppo (uh-LEH-poh) is the second largest city in Syria. Located between the Euphrates River and the Mediterranean Sea on a rocky cliff in northwestern Syria, this ancient city has survived attacks from many enemies over the centuries. Today, Aleppo is the most industrialized city in Syria. Textile mills are the major industry, but tanneries and food processing plants are also plentiful. The region around Aleppo is highly cultivated, with major crops of wheat, fruit, nuts, and barley.

Other Cities

Few other cities match Damascus and Aleppo in size, but the thriving port of Latakia (laa-tuh-KEE-uh) on the coast of the Mediterranean is vital to the Syrian economy. Homs (HAWMS), located north of Damascus, is the site of one of Syria's first oil refineries in addition to being a major agricultural producer. A gap in the mountains near Homs has made it a major crossroads for centuries. Today, highways and railroads run through the gap, linking the coastal region with the country's interior. Just north of Homs is the city of Hama (HAA-mah), known primarily as the site of the 1982 massacre of an estimated 10,000 people when the Syrian government quelled an uprising by the Islamic extremist group called the Muslim Brotherhood, or Ikhwan.

Climate

Syria's climate varies greatly by region. The coastal region is by far the wettest, with 30 to 40 inches (75 to 100 centimeters) of rain annually—most of it falling in the winter months. Temperatures in the region are moderated by the Mediterranean. Summer highs average 80° F (27° C), while winter temperatures are generally around 45° F (7° C).

The plateau region just east of the mountains is much more arid, since the mountain ranges stop most of the moisture that comes off the Mediterranean Sea. The region receives less than 8 inches (20 centimeters) of precipitation in a typical year. There is a wider temperature swing here than in the coastal plain region. Winter temperatures average 39° F (4° C), while summer temperatures often reach 100° F (38° C).

The desert region of eastern Syria is known for meager rainfall—less than 4 inches (10 centimeters) annually—as well as for summertime temperatures that often soar above 109° F (43° C). Seasonal winds create blinding sandstorms in February and May, bringing everything in the region to a halt until they end.

In northeastern Syria, near the Euphrates River, about 10 inches (25 centimeters) of precipitation falls each year. Severe frosts are common in the region during the winter months.

A rare winter snow near Damascus in 2003 provides entertainment for a group of Syrian boys. Damascus is located in the southwestern corner of Syria, to the east of the mountains. This region is generally dry, with temperatures that stay above the freezing mark.

Natural Resources

Syria's economy depends upon its oil and natural gas reserves. The most productive reserves are located in northeastern Syria. Although oil has been produced since the 1960s, it wasn't until 2000 that Syria began working with energy companies to develop the natural gas reserves in the country. This diversification was necessary, since the oil reserves are quickly nearing depletion.

Syria's fertile land is another of its most important natural resources. Cotton and wheat are valuable crops in Syria, as are potatoes, sugar beets, and tobacco. Citrus and olive trees are also grown but not in large quantities. In the 1960s, the government established agricultural cooperatives, hoping to dilute the power of major landowners while educating Syrian farmers on the latest agricultural methods. Unfortunately, the cooperatives have demonstrated few gains in productivity.

Plants and Animals

Syria's hot, dry climate does not produce enough vegetation to support much wildlife. In remote areas, deer, wolves, foxes, badgers, wildcats,

The damascene rose (rose of Damascus), pictured here, is known by flower experts for its beauty and aroma. It can blossom for up to a month and a half each spring.

IMPORTANT EVENTS IN SYRIA'S HISTORY

3000 B.C.E. The Amorites and Canaanites settle in Greater Syria.

1600 B.C.E. The Egyptians conquer much of Greater Syria.

333 B.C.E. Alexander the Great pushes into the Mediterranean region and conquers the Persian Empire.

64 B.C.E. Hadrian leads Roman armies into Greater Syria and conquers the region.

324 C.E. Constantine the Great converts to Christianity and establishes the Byzantine Empire.

610 The Prophet Mohammad begins preaching Islam.

635 Islamic armies introduce the new religion in Greater Syria.

661 Muawiyah establishes the Umayyad Dynasty, which rules over the Islamic world for the next nine decades.

1094 Seljuk Turks conquer the Hamdani kingdom and establish Shi'a rule over the area.

1099 The Crusaders capture Jerusalem and establish a Christian kingdom.

1187 Saladin, the great Muslim warrior, leads his armies against the Crusaders and regains control of Jerusalem.

1516 The Ottomans invade Greater Syria, defeating the Mamluks.

1916 The British ask the Hashemite family of Mecca to lead an Arab rebellion against the Ottomans.

1918 Faisal gains control of Greater Syria.

1920 Faisal is crowned king of Syria, but isn't recognized by France or Britain. The League of Nations awards France a mandate to rule over Syria.

1926 The French separate Lebanon from Syria and make each a distinct country.

1928 The Nationalist Bloc political party forms.

1936 Syria and France sign a treaty placing a nationalist government in charge of Syria.

1941 Free French troops occupy Syria and announce that independence will be granted soon.

1943 Syrians elect Shukri al-Quwatly to serve as their first president.

1944 The United States and the Soviet Union recognize Syria as an independent nation.

1945 Britain recognizes Syria's independence, but France balks.

1946 France finally evacuates Syria on April 17, a date now celebrated as a national holiday.

1958 Egypt and Syria join together to form the United Arab Republic (UAR).

1961 Syria secedes from the UAR.

1963 The Baath Party seizes control of the Syrian government.

1967 Israel captures Syria's Golan Heights territory during the Six-Day War.

1970 Hafez al-Assad becomes Syria's president following a coup.

1973 Syria and Egypt attack Israel, trying to regain control of their occupied territories.

1976 Syria sends troops to Lebanon to intervene in the civil war there.

1982 Assad orders an attack on Hama in an effort to crush a rebellion by the Muslim Brotherhood.

1991 Syria holds peace talks with Israel but no agreement is reached.

2000 President Hafez al-Assad dies and is succeeded by his son, Bashar al-Assad.

2001 Syria withdraws some of its troops from Beirut, leaving 20,000 soldiers in Lebanon.

2003 Syria orders the withdrawal of an additional 3,500 troops from Lebanon and announces plans for a full withdrawal in 2004.

and *martens*—small mammals that are related to weasels—can still be found. Lizards and chameleons are common in the desert region, while eagles and buzzards are often seen in the mountains.

Two domesticated animals are highly valued in Syria: the mule and the camel. People in the mountains depend upon the mule, while the camel carries food and supplies in the desert. Farming families often raise livestock such as cows, chickens, horses, sheep, and goats.

History

Ancient Days

People have lived in Greater Syria for thousands of years, although little is known about them prior to 3000 B.C.E. (Historic Syria is often called Greater Syria. It included present-day Syria, Lebanon, Jordan, Israel, and part of Turkey.) Around then, the Amorites—Semitic nomads from the Arabian Peninsula—established settlements near the Euphrates River, in an area known as the Fertile Crescent. The ancient trading kingdom of Ebla flourished in the region south of Aleppo. The Phoenicians, descendants of the Canaanites who were known for their sailing and trading prowess, flourished along the Mediterranean coast. The Egyptians often traveled to Greater Syria to harvest the abundant cedar, pine, and cypress that grew in the mountains.

> *Did You Know?*
>
> The Phoenicians got their name from a rare purple dye that they harvested from mollusks along the coast of Syria. Because only the wealthy could afford the dye, purple became known as the color of royalty. The Phoenicians also developed the first alphabet, which contained thirty letters.

These early Syrians prospered as commercial trading routes developed between Mesopotamia (present-day Iraq), Egypt, Anatolia (present-day Turkey), and the Mediterranean coast of Syria. Their wealth drew a succession of conquerors, including the Akkadians and Babylonians from Mesopotamia. By 1600 B.C.E., the Egyptians controlled much of Greater Syria.

The Egyptians held power for two centuries before the Assyrians and Hittites invaded the region from the north. Over time, the Hittites established settlements in northern and central Greater Syria. In the thirteenth century B.C.E., the Aramaeans (ahr-uh-MEE-uns), wealthy merchants who traded with the people of the Arabian Peninsula, founded a kingdom that included the cities of Damascus and Aleppo. Their language—Aramaic (ahr-uh-MAY-ik)—quickly became the common language in Greater Syria. Traders throughout the Middle East used Aramaic to communicate, and it was spoken extensively in the Persian Empire.

As the northern Assyrian Empire grew in power, it launched constant attacks against the kingdoms in Greater Syria. By 732 B.C.E.,

This statue, from the ninth century B.C.E., depicts an Aramaean king. The Aramaeans, a group of wealthy merchants, established a kingdom that included Damascus in the thirteenth century B.C.E. Their language quickly became the common language throughout Syria.

Assyrians ruled Greater Syria, but their control lasted only until 572, when the Babylonians (also known as the Chaldeans) conquered Greater Syria. Babylonian rule ended in 538 B.C.E., when the Persian Empire rampaged through the region. Under the Persians, the Syrians regained some degree of independence, but they would remain under foreign control until the twentieth century.

Western Influence

In 333 B.C.E., Alexander the Great—one of history's greatest conquerors—crushed the Persian Empire and introduced Greek culture into the region. Alexander died a decade later, and control over Greater Syria passed down to one of his generals. Seleucus and his descendants,

After the death of Alexander the Great, the great Greek conqueror, in the fourth century B.C.E., control of Greater Syria was passed to Seleucus, pictured in this engraving. The Seleucids, as his descendants were known, ruled the area for three hundred years.

known as the Seleucids, ruled over Greater Syria for three hundred years. During this time, many Greeks settled in Syria. New trading routes to India, Europe, and China were developed, ensuring the kingdom's continued prosperity. The Greeks introduced the teachings of their learned philosophers and scientists and were in turn influenced by Eastern thought.

The Romans invaded Greater Syria in the first century B.C.E. under the leadership of the emperor Hadrian and conquered the region in 64 B.C.E. Cities such as Damascus and Palmyra (present-day Tadmor) continued to flourish under Roman rule. Many of the roads and aqueducts that were built by the Romans are still in use today.

The Byzantine Era

In 324 C.E., the Roman emperor Constantine the Great converted to Christianity. He established a capital in the city of Byzantium, renaming it Constantinople (present-day Istanbul, Turkey). The eastern Roman provinces became known as the Byzantine Empire and included Greater Syria.

Under Byzantine rule, many Syrians living in the north and in the cities became Christians. Around the seventh century, the Sassanian Persian Empire stepped up its attacks on Greater Syria, capturing Jerusalem in 611. Many of the Christian Arab tribes living on the eastern plateau acted as guards for the region and were supported by the Byzantines. Although the Byzantines eventually recaptured Jerusalem, they no longer had enough money to support the Arabs guarding the frontier. Many scholars believe this left Greater Syria vulnerable to the Islamic armies that would soon sweep northward.

The Advent of Islam

At the beginning of the seventh century, the Prophet Mohammad began preaching a new religion, called Islam, in Arabia. Islamic armies spread the new religion across Arabia. Some armies swept northward, invading and conquering Greater Syria in 635.

Following Mohammad's death in 632, his followers selected *caliphs* (spiritual and political leaders) to rule over the growing Islamic empire. The first three caliphs ruled from Mecca (in present-day Saudi Arabia), but power eventually shifted northward.

Muawiyah, a member of the Umayyad clan, proclaimed himself caliph after the assassination of Ali, the fourth caliph, in 661. Already the governor of Syria, Muawiyah established the caliphate in Damascus. Under his rule, the Islamic empire continued to expand. Christians and Jews were allowed to continue following their own religions, although they had to pay a tax to do so. Christians were recruited to serve in the army and held government office during Muawiyah's reign.

The period of rule by Muawiyah and his successors became known as the Umayyad dynasty. The Umayyads ruled over the Islamic world for nearly nine decades. During this time, Damascus and other Syrian cities prospered. Foreign trade grew, and great strides were made in the fields of medicine and other sciences. Gradually, Arabic replaced Aramaic as the language of the land.

Political Upheaval

Over time, the Umayyads' authority declined and another Islamic dynasty—the Abbasids—rose to power in 750. The Abbasids moved the Islamic capital from Damascus to Baghdad (in present-day Iraq). Syria received little attention from the Abbasids, and as a result, city-states began to form once again. One of the strongest was the Hamdani kingdom, established by Abu Ali Hasan in Aleppo in the tenth century. Under the leadership of Hasan, the kingdom recorded many achievements in science and literature. In 1094, the Hamdani

SALADIN

Salah al-Din ibn Ayyub, or Saladin, is the most respected Muslim warriors in history. Known for his honor and dignity as well as his military prowess, Saladin became known as the "flower of Islamic chivalry."

Saladin leads his men into battle in this illustration.

kingdom—along with the rest of Greater Syria—fell to the Seljuk Turks, Shi'ite Muslims from the northeast.

Another Shi'a Dynasty, the Fatimids, rose to power in Egypt about the same time. Fatimid armies moved northward and occupied much of southern Syria (present-day Lebanon). Under the leadership of Abu Ali Mansur al-Hakim, the Fatimids destroyed many Christian churches and villages. The Druze religion was established by followers of al-Hakim, who believed that he was an incarnation of God.

In 1095, Pope Urban II called for Christians to travel to the Holy Land (Palestine) and help the Byzantines, who were under attack by Muslim forces. The venture became known as the First Crusade. Both professional armies and ragtag gangs of peasants set out for the Holy Land. The Crusaders gained control of Jerusalem—a city that is holy to

The Fatimid Dynasty rose to power in Egypt in the eleventh century C.E. Its armies moved north and occupied much of southern Syria (present-day Lebanon), establishing the Druze religion. This illustration from the tenth, eleventh, or twelfth century shows Fatimids playing a game with sticks.

Jews, Christians, and Muslims—in 1099, massacring nearly all the Jews and Muslims living in the city. The Muslims regrouped under Salah al-Din ibn Ayyub, known in the West as Saladin (SA-luh-deen). Saladin's forces united Egypt and Syria, conquered many Syrian cities under Crusader control, then recaptured Jerusalem in 1187. Following this success, Saladin founded the Ayyubid Dynasty, which ruled over Egypt and its territories (including Greater Syria) until the mid-thirteenth century. The Mamluks, former slaves who rose to head an Islamic elite that replaced the Ayyubids, ruled over Syria from 1250 until the Ottoman invasion in 1516.

This is the minaret, or tower, of the Ummayad Mosque in the Old City of Damascus. The mosque was built in 705 C.E., during the Umayyad Dynasty. Muawiyah, the leader of the Umayyads, established Damascus as the capital of Islam.

The Ottoman Empire

The Ottomans, Muslim Turks originally from central Asia, established the beginning of their empire in northwestern Anatolia at the start of the fourteenth century. They rapidly expanded their territory, conquering all the Byzantine lands in Europe, including the Byzantine capital of Constantinople, by the mid-1400s. In the course of the sixteenth century, they occupied most of the Middle East and North Africa.

In 1516, the Ottoman Empire invaded Greater Syria and defeated the Mamluks. The area was divided into a number of provinces, the most important with their capitals in Aleppo and Damascus. Each had its own governor, or *pasha,* who was charged with collecting taxes and maintaining order in the name of the Ottoman sultan in Istanbul.

The population of the Syrian cities expanded in the sixteenth century, and Aleppo in particular grew to become a major center of trade with the East as well as with Europe. In the seventeenth and eighteenth centuries, Ottoman central control weakened and insecurity in the Syrian countryside led many villagers to desert their fields. In the nineteenth century, however, the Ottoman government centralized its control, and cultivation was restored in the rural areas. Ottoman reforms in education, health, and other areas benefited Syrians and improved the quality of life in the region.

Brief Freedom

As World War I (1914–1918) began, Ottoman rule became more and more oppressive. Syrians began to embrace the idea of Arab nationalism while calling for reform within the Ottoman government and greater autonomy for the Arabs within the empire. The Arab nationalist movement was introduced by Syrian intellectuals who advocated the study of Arab history, literature, and language. In 1916, British military leaders negotiated with Sharif Hussein, head of the Hashemite family and keeper of the holy city of Mecca, to lead an Arab rebellion against the Ottomans. In return, the British offered to support the creation of an independent Arab state. Hussein's son, Faisal, led an Arab army against the Ottomans, eventually defeating them. In 1918, Faisal took control of most of Syria and appointed a General Syrian Congress. The congress declared Greater Syria to be a free and independent Arab nation. A year later, the General Syrian Congress named Faisal king of Syria.

Faisal's rule went unrecognized by some European nations including France and Great Britain. Ultimately, the League of Nations gave France a *mandate* (commission to govern) over Syria and Lebanon. The remainder of Greater Syria—Palestine (including present-day Israel) and Transjordan—was placed under a British mandate. Faisal fled to Europe, but was later named king of Iraq by the British.

The French Mandate

The French began their rule over Syria by defining administrative districts that separated the Druze, Alawites, and Sunnis. This had the effect of weakening the Arab nationalist movement. The present-day borders of Lebanon were established when the French carved a Christian-dominated state out of part of Syria.

Although the French made much-needed improvements to Syria's *infrastructure* by building roads and schools, their rule was oppressive.

French troops gathered in Syria in 1925 to put down a rebellion by the Druze, a religious sect.
France had gained control in 1918 when it was given a mandate by the League of Nations
to rule Syria and Lebanon after the defeat of the Ottoman Empire.

The French language was taught in all schools, political activity was banned, and civil rights were suppressed. Continual revolts by the individual religious groups resulted in few changes by the French. Finally, in 1925, a revolt by the Druze erupted into a full-fledged rebellion when their forces invaded Damascus. The French bombed Damascus in an effort to end the rebellion, killing 5,000 Syrians.

Once order had been restored, the French made some concessions to the Syrians. A political party called the National Bloc was established in 1928. It supported a new constitution that unified Syria and ended French rule. The French did not accept this constitution, however. It wasn't until 1936, following the adoption of a new treaty, that France gave up any of its power to rule. It continued to hold the ultimate authority in Syria, however.

Independence at Last

World War II began in 1939, and within a year, German forces occupied France, supported by the French Vichy government. French troops that didn't support the Vichy government—the Free French forces—fought with British and Arab troops in the Middle East. By 1941, Free French troops were occupying Syria and Lebanon. With a promise of independence soon to come, the Syrians elected Shukri al-Quwatly president in 1943. Within a year, the United States and the Soviet Union had officially recognized Syria and Lebanon as independent nations.

As the war ended in 1945, Britain granted recognition of Syria's and Lebanon's independence. Syria joined the United Nations (UN) and the Arab League. However, France still refused to withdraw its troops. Instead, it launched attacks on Damascus, Homs, and Hama. In 1946, under threat of military action by Britain and following the passage of a UN resolution ordering France to evacuate Syria, French troops finally withdrew from Syria.

The years immediately following Syria's independence were not easy. The many different factions within Syria, both religious and political, struggled to gain power, and the result was several years of political instability. Governments were established, then quickly overthrown—usually by military leaders.

In the 1950s, Syria developed a close relationship with the Soviet Union. This association was in response to what Syrians viewed as

> **Did You Know?**
> Syrian women were granted the right to vote soon after independence.

Western dishonesty, illustrated by the perceived betrayal of the British at the end of World War I, French actions during the mandate period, and Western support for the creation of Israel.

The United Arab Republic

In the late 1950s, a new political party gained power. The Baath (bah-AHTH) Party, whose name means "renaissance" or "revival," attracted many followers with its Arab nationalist views and demands for social rights. By 1957, it controlled the Syrian government. The *Communist* Party presented a growing threat to the Baathists' power. To counter this threat, the Baathists proposed a federation with Egypt. Egyptian president Gamal Abdel Nasser agreed, and the United Arab Republic (UAR) was established in 1958. Syrians were quickly disillusioned with the new arrangement, however, because Egypt dominated the union, placing its own politicians in Syrian posts. In 1961, Syria seceded from the UAR. Once again, a period of political instability rocked Syria.

The Reemergence of the Baath Party

In 1963, Baathist military officers staged a coup and seized control of the government. Land reform was a top priority, and many wealthy landowners were exiled after their land was appropriated by the government. In 1967, war broke out between Israel and several Arab nations. Syria, Egypt, Iraq, and Jordan had just completed a mutual defense pact, which Israel interpreted as the forerunner to attacks upon its territory. To prevent such attacks, Israel launched decisive military attacks against Egyptian troops in the Sinai Peninsula. When Syria, Iraq, and Jordan joined the fighting, Israel invaded Syria and captured the Golan Heights region south of Damascus. This war became known as the Six-Day War.

Hafez al-Assad, an Alawite military officer and the Syrian minister of defense, led an overthrow of the government in 1970 and was named president of Syria a year later. Although the Sunni majority was dismayed to see an Alawite as president, Assad's firm rule of Syria helped restore order to the fractured nation.

In 1973, Syria and Egypt attacked Israel in what became known as the Yom Kippur War, or the Arab-Israeli War of 1973. Although Syria was initially successful in pushing its troops into Israel, Israel regrouped and soon regained control of the Golan Heights. Israel still occupies this territory today.

South of Syria, a violent civil war broke out in Lebanon in 1975. Syria sent troops to intervene the following year. At first, the Syrian troops acted as peacekeepers and mediators, but soon they were drawn into the fighting, launching attacks against the Palestine Liberation Organization (PLO) and the Christian militias. Israel, whose government was allied with the Christians in Lebanon, also sent troops to intervene in the war. Israeli and Syrian troops often fought against one another in Lebanon. Although Lebanon and Israel agreed in 1983 that all foreign troops should withdraw from the conflict, Syria refused to end its military presence there.

In addition to Syria's involvement in foreign wars, Assad had to deal with fundamentalist groups that were creating unrest within Syria. In 1982, when the Muslim Brotherhood (also called the Ikhwan) launched a rebellion in Hama, Assad ordered the military to bomb the city. At least 10,000 people are thought to have been killed in the attack, and the city was almost completely destroyed. The Muslim Brotherhood was shattered, and few groups rose in its place to threaten Assad's government.

Syrian president Hafez al-Assad (center) is pictured with Egyptian president Hosni Mubarak (left) and Crown Prince Abdullah of Saudi Arabia in June 1996. The three were calling for a summit of Middle East leaders to ensure that peace talks with Israel would continue.

Syria Today

For the past decade, Syria has been working to resolve conflicts with Israel and Lebanon. In 1991, Syria joined other Arab nations to hold peace talks with Israel. Syria had hoped to resolve the lingering

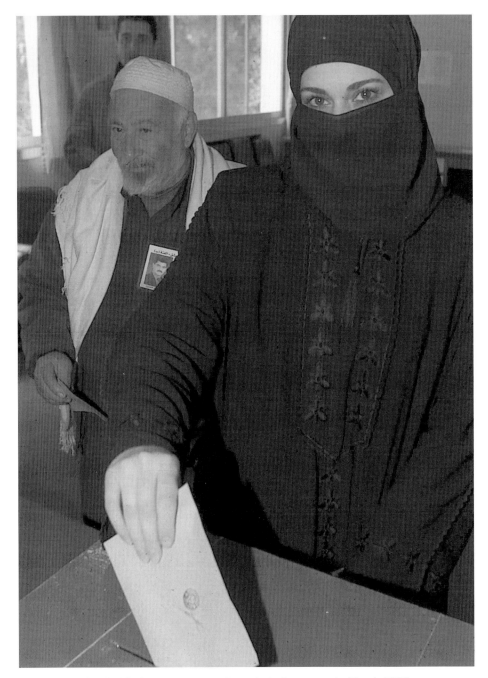

A veiled Syrian woman casts her vote in Damascus in March 2003, in the first parliamentary (legislative) elections in Syria since Bashar al-Assad took office in 2000 after the death of his father.

occupation of the Golan Heights area by Israeli troops, but no agreement was reached. Syria remained in Lebanon following the end of the civil war in 1990 despite Lebanon's request that Syrian troops be withdrawn. After much negotiation, some Syrian troops withdrew from Lebanon in 2001 and 2003. Syria has announced its plans to withdraw all troops from Lebanon in 2004.

Hafez al-Assad died in 2000 and was succeeded by his son, Bashar al-Assad. The government has recently clamped down on gatherings by political parties and on free speech, and there have been new restrictions placed on the press.

Relations between the United States and Syria have grown increasingly strained in recent years. The United States has accused Syria of supporting terrorists. Following the terrorist attacks in New York City and Washington, D.C., on September 11, 2001, U.S. president George W. Bush labeled Syria a "rogue state," charging that Syria was attempting to develop chemical weapons and other weapons of mass destruction. In 2003, as the United States prepared for war in Iraq, government officials accused Syria of providing weapons to Iraq. Syria has denied these charges.

Economy

Agriculture, oil and natural gas production, and manufacturing are the three major revenue producers in the Syrian economy, but the country is still dependent upon aid from other Middle Eastern countries. In the 1990s, Syria defied the economic *sanctions* placed on Iraq by the UN, letting Iraq ship and sell oil through Syrian pipelines and earning a healthy profit in return.

Business and Industry

Syria's fertile soil and irrigation systems enable farmers to produce enough cotton and other crops to meet national needs as well as for export. Overfarming and lack of fertilizers have exhausted the soil in many areas, however.

Oil quickly became a major source of revenue in the late 1960s, when pipelines connecting the oil fields and refineries were completed. However, uncertain oil prices and the probable depletion of known oil reserves in the near future have forced the Syrian government to diversify the economy.

One of the strongest pushes has been in the manufacturing sector. The textile industry has traditionally been strong in Syria, but food processing and tobacco manufacturers expanded in the 1990s. Most industries in Syria are owned and run by the government. In an effort to strengthen the economy, President Bashar al-Assad has invited foreign investment in Syria.

One of the areas with the most potential for economic growth is tourism. Currently, few tourists visit Syria despite its wealth of historical sites.

Media and Communications

Most newspapers, radio, and television stations in Syria are owned by the government. After Bashar al-Assad became president in 2000, rules were relaxed, allowing privately owned newspapers to be published for

Although Bashar al-Assad has relaxed some rules regarding the media in Syria, there are still many restrictions on what can and cannot be printed, broadcast, or viewed on the Internet. This man in Damascus peruses a Syrian magazine.

the first time since the Baath Party came to power in the 1960s. Licensing requirements were soon instituted, however, making it easier for the government to shut down any publication that criticized the president, his family, or the government. Privately owned radio stations were allowed in 2002, but the broadcast content is highly restricted; no news or political commentary is permitted.

When Assad took office, he announced his commitment to providing Internet service to Syria. Today, there are two Internet cafes in Syria, both owned by the government. Access to Web sites is restricted, however. Sites that present the views of countries that Syria considers enemies, such as Israel, are blocked, as are sites that criticize the Syrian government and those that do not meet Islamic guidelines.

Religion and Beliefs

Although there are two main religious groups in Syria—Muslims and Christians—each group has many sects with differing beliefs. The Islamic community is made up primarily of Sunnis, Alawites, and Ismailis, while the Christian community includes Eastern Orthodox sects, Catholics, and a small number of Protestants. A small percentage of Syrians follow the Druze religion, a mysterious sect that is believed to combine aspects from Islamic, Christian, and pagan religions. Although there was once a sizable Jewish community in Syria, all but a handful of Jews have emigrated to other countries.

Islam

Muslims follow the teachings of the Prophet Mohammad, who established Islam in the seventh century. They believe in one God—Allah—the same God of the Jews and Christians. According to Islamic tradition, God revealed the Qur'an, the Muslim holy book (more commonly called the Koran in the West) to Mohammad, the last in a series of prophets that includes Abraham and Jesus. Devout Muslims observe the five pillars or duties of Islam: professing that "there is no God but God and Mohammad is his messenger," praying five times daily, fasting during the holy month of Ramadan, giving alms (charity) to the poor, and making a pilgrimage to Mecca, the birthplace of Mohammad at least once in their lifetime.

Following Mohammad's death, the Islamic community was divided about how to select a caliph, or successor. Most believed that the community as a whole should select the caliph. Some believed that leadership of the Islamic community should go to Ali, Mohammad's son-in-law and cousin and his descendants. Over the next century, this disagreement deepened. Eventually, the traditionalists became known as Sunni Muslims, while those who believed that Ali and his descendants were the rightful Islamic leaders were called Shi'a Muslims or Shi'ites. (To learn more about Islam, see pages ix–xii in the introduction to this volume.)

Within the Shi'ite community, further differences developed. Most Shi'ites believed that there were twelve *imams*, religious leaders descended from Mohammad and Ali that had divine authority to interpret the Qur'an. These Shi'ites were known as the Jafari, or Twelver, Shi'ites. Others in the Shi'ite community—the Ismailis—traced the descendants of Ali differently, recognizing seven imams.

In Syria, an offshoot of the Twelver Shi'ite community developed in the mountains of Jabal an-Nusayriyah. First known as Nusayris, this community later became known as the Alawites. They believe that Mohammad's son-in-law Ali was also a prophet and, as such, was the rightful successor to Mohammad. While they recognize the five pillars of Islam, Alawites believe that these are symbolic rather than required duties. They also add two additional pillars: *jihad*, or struggle, and *waliya*, loyalty to Ali.

In addition to observing Islamic holidays such as Eid al-Fitr and Eid al-Adha, the Alawites celebrate the Christian holy days of Christmas and Epiphany. They also observe No-Ruz, an ancient celebration of spring and the New Year that originated with the Zoroastrians of Iran. Because of their observance of other religious traditions and their refusal to treat the five pillars of Islam as religious duties, most mainstream Muslims do not consider the Alawites to be Muslims. Although the Alawites are in the minority in Syria, they have ruled the country for over four decades.

Christianity

The Christian religion grew out of Judaism about 2,000 years ago in Israel, when Jesus Christ began teaching about faith and God's love. Christians believe that Jesus Christ is the son of God. They believe that Jesus was resurrected after his death and that they too can have eternal life because of their faith in Jesus. Although Jews, Christians, and Muslims all worship the same God, Christians believe that God exists as three persons—the Father, the Son, and the Holy Spirit. This is sometimes called the Holy Trinity.

Leaders of the early Christian churches, called bishops, met regularly to define the Christian doctrine, or beliefs. Early in the eleventh century,

Gregarious the Third, a Roman Catholic leader in Syria, holds an Easter mass in Damascus in 2003. Many Christian Easter celebrations in Syria that year were low-key, as a way of showing support for fellow Arabs in Iraq, which was then under attack from the United States at the time.

the Roman bishop—known as the pope—claimed that his office had complete authority from God to govern all the churches and define the church doctrine. Bishops of the churches in Asia disagreed. They believed that churches should govern themselves and that the pope had no more divine authority than the other bishops. The churches that followed the pope became known as Roman Catholic churches, while those that repudiated the pope's claims joined together as Eastern Orthodox churches. Both groups have sects that differ slightly in their religious practices. In the sixteenth century, a Roman Catholic monk named Martin Luther protested many of the church teachings, charging that church leaders were corrupting the religion. The churches he founded became known as Protestant churches. Today there are many different Protestant churches, each with its own beliefs. (For more information about Christianity, see pages 53–55, 56–60 in Volume 1 of this series.)

Did You Know?

Syrians in the predominantly Christian village of Maaloula still speak Aramaic, the language spoken by Jesus Christ.

Christianity spread to Syria very soon after Christ's death. After the split in church leadership in the eleventh century, both Orthodox and Catholic churches were established in Syria. Today, the Orthodox community includes members of the Greek Orthodox, Armenian Orthodox, and Syrian Orthodox churches. There are several small congregations of Catholics as well, including Syrian, Greek, Chaldean, Maronite, Latin, and Armenian Catholic.

Druze

The Druze religion began in Egypt in the eleventh century as an offshoot of Shi'a Islam. Little is known about the specific beliefs of the Druze because their worship traditions are not shared with outsiders. The Druze do not convert others to their faith, and they do not marry outside of their religious community.

Elements of both Christianity and pagan religions are present in Druze religious practices. The Druze incorporate mysticism into their worship, and they believe in reincarnation. In their religious view, God has appeared on earth in human form at several points in history, including as Jesus Christ and Mohammad. The Druze believe that the last incarnation of God was al-Hakim, the leader of the Islamic Fatimid Dynasty in Egypt.

Syria has the largest Druze population in the world, followed by Lebanon.

Everyday Life

Everyday life varies greatly among different social groups in Syria, depending upon where people live and their economic level. Educated professionals living in the cities enjoy many of the same amenities found in Western cities, while many poor families follow *Bedouin* customs, such as covering the walls and floor with handwoven rugs and designating separate rooms for men and women when they visit with friends. Much of the housing in the warm regions is still built in the traditional manner, formed of mud and straw into a beehive shape. In the cities, wealthier citizens live in homes built of stone, while the Bedouins still live in tents. Village homes are likely to be made of bricks

Syrians enjoy a courtyard café in the Old City of Damascus. The café occupies one of the thousands of old houses in the Old City that feature central, open courtyards, often with pools in the middle. While many modern city-dwellers live in newer homes, some of these older homes are being renovated.

and plaster, with one to three rooms. Most Syrians have electricity and indoor plumbing in their homes.

Modern technology has had an impact on Syrian lifestyles at every level, however. The most striking example is that of the Bedouins, who traditionally herded their camels and sheep between summer and winter grazing spots. While few still follow the nomadic lifestyle, those who do are likely to transport their herds between grazing grounds in a pickup or trailer. Portable generators allow televisions to be used at any location.

Family Life

Life in Syria continues to revolve around family. Decisions are always considered in light of the effect they will have on the family unit as a whole, rather than an individual. In this context, it is not surprising that arranged marriages are still very common in Syria. A good match is one that benefits both families involved. Most young Syrians regard getting married and raising a family as a high priority.

A Syrian family drives past the Roman ruins in Palmyra, north of Damascus, in their open-air vehicle. Family life is an important priority for Syrians. Arranged marriages are still common, since the welfare of the family is more important than the personal choice of the individual.

In some villages, large families—with as many as twelve children—
are still commonplace. This is due both to religious beliefs and the
rigors of farm life; the more children a family has, the more help they
can provide with farmwork. According to Islamic law, men may have up
to four wives as long as they are treated equally. This practice is
declining, although it is more common in the villages than in the cities.

Since Syria's independence, there has been an emphasis on
improving conditions for women. Women have been given the right to
vote. Many women work as doctors, lawyers, teachers, and engineers. A
few women are in politics. However, these women belong to the wealthy
classes. The condition of poor women has not shown a great deal of
improvement.

Dress

Dress styles are quite diverse in Syria. Clothing varies according to
family custom, religion, and where people live. Most Muslim women
wear Western clothing with a white veil covering their hair. However, in
small towns and villages, it is not unusual to see conservative Muslim
women wearing a long black coat that covers their clothing and a black
veil that covers their hair and face.

Some men and boys wear jeans and shirts. Others wear traditional
Arab clothing, including an ankle-length tunic and headdress. The
headdress has three parts: a small cap called a *tajia*; the *ghutra,* a square
cloth that covers the *tajia*; and an *agal* (ah-GAHL)—the black cord that
holds the *ghutra* in place.

Many wealthy and educated Syrians dress similarly to Americans or
Europeans. The Bedouins have their own hand-embroidered designs
and often wear brightly colored clothing.

Education

The Syrian government provides a free education for its citizens, and all
children are required to attend school until age eleven. Most boys
continue their education through high school, and many continue on to
college. However, many girls in the villages leave school after sixth grade
because their parents want them to help take care of the family and
farm. In recent decades, there has been an increase in the number of
Muslim women who are continuing their education through the
university level.

There are universities in Damascus, Aleppo, and Latakia, as well as the Institute of Petroleum at Homs. In the last decade, technical and trade schools have opened to train students for secretarial and mechanical occupations. The Syrian government encourages its citizens to further their education in other countries but is concerned about a "brain drain"—the departure of educated professionals from their native country in search of higher wages or a more stable political environment, leaving the home country without the expertise or experience it needs in key posts. Therefore the Syrian government makes every effort to keep its educated citizens in Syria.

Recreation and Leisure

Most Syrians work eight to ten hours a day, six days a week, leaving little free time for leisure activities. Most social activities involve the whole family. Lunch or dinner with family and friends is a favorite social event.

Public speaking, especially reciting the Qur'an and poetry from memory, is a major source of entertainment. These oral traditions have been passed down through the centuries and are still vital among nomads today.

Sports are favorite pastimes for many Syrians. Soccer (called football in Syria) and basketball are very popular in the large cities. Swimming is a favorite summertime activity. Wrestling is also becoming widely popular in Syria.

People in the cities have greater access to leisure activities than those in small towns. Movie theaters showing films from the United States, Europe, and India attract many viewers in Damascus and Aleppo. Nightclubs are very popular with younger people, while concerts featuring musical styles ranging from jazz to classical draw music lovers of all ages.

Food

Syrians delight in preparing delicious foods that are beautifully presented. While traditional Syrian cuisine has much in common with other Middle Eastern countries, the ingredients are often presented in new combinations. Because Syria has a large Muslim population, pork and alcohol, which are prohibited by the Qur'an, are not eaten by most Syrians. The sale of alcohol is not prohibited, however, and some areas—particularly around Aleppo and Homs—are known for their wines and *arak,* an anise-flavored brandy.

A typical day begins quite early in Syrian households. Muslim families rise before dawn for morning prayers. Following a light breakfast of cheese, yogurt, and coffee, family members go to work and

A vendor in a Damascus souk, or market, offers a beverage known as tamarind from a dispenser worn on his back. Tamarind, a healthy drink made from the fruit of the tamarind tree, is popular throughout the Arab world.

school. Lunch, served in the early afternoon, is typically the largest meal of the day. The meal begins with meze, a collection of appetizers such as cucumbers, olives, *baba ghanoush* (a dip made from roasted eggplants), and *hummus* (a puree of chickpeas and sesame seed paste). Meat dishes, usually made with lamb or chicken, are served with vegetables, bread, and fruit. *Tabbouleh*—a salad made with bulgar wheat, herbs, onions, and tomatoes—is another favorite dish.

Trays of olives and sour pickles are served at the end of the meal, as is Turkish coffee or tea. Most businesses close during the heat of the afternoon, so families are able to rest after lunch. Dinner, which is eaten late, is generally very light.

Fresh ingredients are used for each meal, requiring daily trips to many different shops, since each specializes in a different type of food. A typical shopping trip might include stops at the butcher for

In the Souk al Hamidiya in Damascus, one of the oldest markets in the Arab world, a young vendor carries a board of traditional Arabic flat bread on his head. Flat breads and other baked goods can also be purchased at the many bakeries throughout Syria.

meat, the grocer for canned goods, the fruit and vegetable stands, and the bakery. Most bakeries specialize, with some making only traditional Syrian sweets, while others sell Arab flat breads, rolls and baguettes, cakes, or pastries.

Syrians love sweets—candies, pastries, and cakes are highly regarded throughout the country. Each region and city has its own specialty—different kinds of cake or preserved fruits or pastry. Syrian candies are so sweet that a person usually eats only one or two small pieces. Sour foods—such as sour pickles and unripe fruits and nuts—provide a welcome contrast to the sweets.

Syrians have one of the highest sugar consumptions per capita in the world.

Hospitality is an integral part of the Syrian culture, developed over centuries of believing that an individual would bring dishonor to the family by refusing a guest—even an enemy—food and drink. As a result, meals are often transformed into social events lasting two or three hours. Guests are expected to eat until the food is gone, since refusing food is considered very rude.

HUMMUS

Hummus is a dip made of chickpeas and sesame seed paste that is enjoyed throughout the Arab world.

1 cup dried chickpeas
   (also called garbanzo beans)
1 teaspoon baking soda
3/4 cup tahini (sesame seed paste)
Salt, to taste
Juice of 2 lemons, or to taste
1 clove garlic, crushed
Paprika and olive oil, for garnish

Soak the dried chickpeas overnight in a large bowl filled with water to which the baking soda has been added. Drain and rinse the chickpeas before cooking.

Place the chickpeas in a saucepan, cover with cold water, and place over medium-high heat. Bring to a boil, then reduce the heat to low and simmer, covered, for 1 to 1-1/2 hours or until very tender.

Drain the chickpeas, reserving the cooking water and a few whole chickpeas. Place the rest of the chickpeas in a food processor. Process to a smooth puree and transfer to a mixing bowl. Stir in the tahini and salt to taste and blend well. Add the lemon juice and the crushed garlic. If the puree is too thick, thin it with a little of the cooking water. The puree should be creamy but not runny. Taste and adjust the seasoning if necessary, then pour into a shallow round or oval bowl. Spread across the dish, raising the puree slightly at the edges. Place the reserved whole chickpeas in the center of the hummus. Sprinkle the raised edges and center with paprika, and trickle a little olive oil between the whole chickpeas.

Serves 4.

Source: Adapted from *Mediterranean Street Food* by Anissa Helou.

Holidays and Festivals

Most of the holidays celebrated in Syria are religious in nature. The Islamic calendar is based on lunar cycles, making it shorter than the Gregorian calendar that is used as an international standard. Because of this difference, Islamic holidays fall on different dates each year.

Islamic Holidays

The feast of Eid al-Fitr, which marks the end of the holy month of Ramadan, is a joyous occasion for all Muslims. It begins at the sighting of the new moon and continues for three days. Family and friends

Syrians can indulge their well-known sweet tooth at bakeries that specialize in sweets. This bakery in the Old City of Damascus prepares for the Eid al-Fitr holiday with mountains of sweet pastries.

gather for feasts that include many special foods and sweets. Children receive gifts of money and are often allowed to stay up all night. Street carnivals and fireworks brighten the evenings and lend a festive air to the occasion.

Eid al-Adha, or the Feast of the Sacrifice, is celebrated at the end of the pilgrimage season. This festival commemorates Abraham's obedience to God. In preparation for the four-day festival, each family slaughters a sheep or goat. As thanks for Allah's mercy in providing a rich bounty for his people, the meat is shared with relatives and the poor.

Parades, festive meals, and fairs are often organized to celebrate the Islamic New Year and the Prophet Mohammad's birthday. Shi'ite Muslims also observe Ashura, a solemn commemoration of the murder of Mohammad's grandson Hussein. This ten-day period of mourning is often marked by special reenactments of Hussein's martyrdom. Some Shi'ite men beat their backs and chests with chains, a ritual that recalls the brutality and torture that Hussein faced before his death.

Christian Celebrations

Advent, Christmas, and Epiphany mark the beginning of the Christian year. Advent is the four-week period leading up to Christmas. During this time, Christians prepare themselves spiritually to celebrate the birth of Jesus Christ. For many Orthodox Christians, this preparation includes a period of fasting. The Christmas season begins with Christmas and ends twelve days later on Epiphany. Traditionally, Epiphany commemorates the Magi, the Three Wise Men who revealed baby Jesus as the son of God.

Christmas celebrations in Syria begin on Christmas Eve. Christians lock their gates as a reminder of the times that they had to worship in secret. Bonfires are lit as families read the story of the birth of Christ and sing Christmas hymns. According to tradition, the manner in which the fire burns predicts how lucky the coming year will be. As the fire dies down, each person makes a wish and jumps over the coals. Church services are held before dawn on Christmas morning to welcome the Christ child. In recent years, it has become more common to see decorated Christmas trees in Syrian homes, although Christmas lights are still rare.

A Syrian legend tells of the Wise Men's long journey to find the Christ Child. A young camel in the caravan, unused to hard travel, was nearing collapse but refused to stop and rest. Because of the camel's strong desire to see the baby Jesus, it was blessed with eternal life. On Epiphany, the Smallest Camel visits well-behaved children and leaves them gifts.

Easter is the other major Christian holiday. Because it celebrates the resurrection of Christ and the promise of eternal life for those who follow his teachings, Easter is the most important day in the Christian calendar.

The forty-day period leading up to Easter is called Lent. Lent is a time of spiritual searching and recommitment. Many Christians abstain from certain foods during all or part of Lent. Holy Week, the week before Easter, begins with Palm Sunday. During Holy Week services, Christians remember Christ's entry into Jerusalem, his betrayal, the last supper with his disciples, and his crucifixion. Easter Sunday is a day of rejoicing when Christians celebrate Christ's resurrection from the dead.

The Arts

Popular art forms such as literature, painting, and music have flourished in Syria throughout history. In addition, Syria is known for its many beautiful traditional crafts.

Traditional Crafts

Syria's traditional arts and crafts include textiles, pottery, metalwork, and glassblowing. Techniques used thousands of years ago have been passed down from generation to generation and are still practiced today.

The textile arts are closely associated with Syria, particularly the brocade cloth called *damask,* named for Damascus. Damask was originally made of silk woven to show a raised design on both sides of the fabric. The silk was often interwoven with gold and silver threads. Today, the damask cloth is made of other fibers as well as silk. Another textile art associated with Syria is the intricate embroidery that

Glassblowing was invented by the Syrians in the first century B.C.E. Their skill is demonstrated by this stained-glass window in the Great Mosque of Damascus. It is topped by an elaborate mosaic of silver and gold.

decorates clothing, table linens, pillows, and other fabric items. The Bedouins are known for their handwoven rugs, especially the small prayer rugs that are laid on the ground so their design points toward Mecca. (Muslims face Mecca during daily prayers.) The Bedouins also make larger rugs that cover the floors of their tents.

Syrian pottery can be found in most souks. Today's artisans mine the same natural clay deposits as ancient potters. While ancient pottery was utilitarian in form, contemporary artists create decorative pieces as well as practical ware.

Syria has a wide range of metals available for artists to work with. Over the centuries, silver, gold, and copper have been made into jewelry and housewares. The elaborate gold and silver filigree jewelry made in Syria is often worn as a status symbol. Those who live in cities tend to wear gold, while Bedouins and villagers wear silver jewelry. Silver is also used to make silverware, trays, and baskets, while brass and copper are used for plates, bowls, pitchers, and coffee servers. Metals are used in wood and stone inlay projects as well.

Glassblowing, another Syrian tradition, was actually invented by the Syrians in the Aleppo area in the first century B.C.E. Both decorative and functional pieces were in high demand, and artists exported their wares throughout the Roman Empire. Although the earliest glassworkers used molds, the Syrians later developed a method of free-form glassblowing. Handblown glass is still made today in factories that date back centuries. It is made in three colors: cobalt blue, green, and amber. The factories create products using one color of glass at a time, rotating the colors every thirty days.

Visual Arts

Because Islam prohibits the representation of people and animals, stylized geometric designs and calligraphy—a style of ornate writing—have developed as the primary art forms. In Damascus, artists create geometric designs by gluing together small slivers of wood. The use of woods of different colors, combined sometimes with metals and shells, creates a decorative mosaic. This art is called *marquetry*. Marquetry artists use small pieces of wood and wood inlay to decorate small boxes, furniture, and buildings.

Music

Syrians enjoy both traditional Arab music and modern music. Traditional musicians play the *oud*—the Arab lute—flutes, fiddles, and drums to accompany songs that tell stories of love and honor. European-style orchestras play modern music. Most modern performing groups include a vocalist and backup chorus.

A Syrian band performs in front of a huge embroidered mural that was exhibited in Damascus in 2002. The mural features the names of Palestinian villages, with red patches used for demolished villages and green patches for villages that still exist. The mural was embroidered by about 1,400 Palestinian and Jordanian people.

Literature

Syria, like other Arab countries, has a rich oral tradition of storytelling and poetry. Poetry continues to be a popular form of expression, and public recitations and readings are common. One famous Syrian poet who has used poetry as an outlet for political beliefs is Ali Ahmad Said, who goes by the pen name of Adonis. His poems tell stories of political strife and urge the need for social change. He was exiled to Beirut in 1956 because of his political views and still lives there today.

Because Syria has a history of repressing free speech, many Syrian writers have settled in neighboring Lebanon. There they explore themes that reflect the unrest of their native country, such as rebellion, struggle, and political and social change.

GLOSSARY

Bedouin Arab nomadic herders who live in the desert

caliph literally, "successor"; used by Muslims as a title for a spiritual and political leader who succeeded Mohammad

communist a person who supports communism, a system of government in which the state plans and controls the economy and a single, often authoritarian party holds power, claiming to make progress toward a higher social order in which all goods are equally shared by the people

coup shortened version of *coup d'état,* the overthrow of a government, usually by a small group

desalination the process by which saltwater is converted to water suitable for drinking and irrigation

hajj pilgrimage to Mecca, one of the five duties required of all Muslims

imam spiritual leader; in Shi'a Islam, the imams are believed to be infallible religious authorities

infrastructure the public works of a country or state, including water purification and energy facilities, transportation, communications, schools, and hospitals

jinn spirits or gods worshiped by many Arabs in the centuries before Islam

mandate commission to govern a region or country, especially after World War I

mutaween the religious police in Saudi Arabia

oasis a green, fertile area that is surrounded by desert (*plural:* oases)

protectorate a relationship in which a strong country agrees to protect a smaller country or region in return for some degree of control over the smaller country's affairs

sanctions punishments, usually economic, that one country or group of countries imposes on another, such as not letting that country buy or sell certain types of goods

ulama Islamic religious leaders

wadi usually dry riverbed that cuts through a desert area

Wahhabism a strict form of Islam established by followers of Muhammad ibn Abd al-Wahhab in the mid-eighteenth century; the official form of Islam in Saudi Arabia today

BIBLIOGRAPHY

Arabicnet.com. "Syria: The Cradle of Civilizations." <http://syria. arabicnet.com/damas.asp>

Associated Press. "Saudi Clerics Hit More Rights for Women." 9/11/03. <http://www.kansascity.com/mld/kansascity/6741701.htm>

———. "Saudi Women Make Strides, But Still Face Barriers." *USA Today.* 5/11/02. <http://www.usatoday.com/news/world/2002/ 05/11/saudi.htm>

BBC News. "U.S. Expands 'Axis of Evil.'" 5/6/02. <http://news.bbc. co.uk/1/hi/world/americas/1971852.stm>

Beaton, Margaret. *Enchantment of the World: Syria.* Chicago: Children's Press, 1988.

Britannica Concise Encyclopedia. "Rub' Al-Khali." Encyclopedia Britannica. 2003. <http://concise.britannica.com/ebc/ article?eu=402574>

Burns, John F. "Arab TV Gets a New Slant: Newscasts Without Censorship." *New York Times.* 7/4/99. <http://www.nytimes.com

Cahoon, Ben M. World Statesman.com. <http://www.worldstatesmen. org/Saudi_Arabia.htm>

Citizenship and Immigration Canada. "Qatar—A Cultural Profile Project." <http://www.settlement.org/cp/english/qatar/index.html>

Collelo, Thomas, ed. *Syria: A Country Study.* Federal Research Division, Library of Congress. Washington, DC: Department of the Army, 1988. <http://lcweb2.loc.gov/frd/cs/sytoc.html>

The Columbia Encyclopedia, 6th ed. "Wahhabi." 2002. <http://www.bartleby.com/65/wa/Wahhabi.html>

Columbus Guides. "Qatar." <http://www.columbusguides.com/data/ qat/qat.asp>

Dosti, Rose. *Mideast & Mediterranean Cuisines*. Tucson, AZ: Fisher Books, 1993.

Egan, W.C. "Christmas in Syria." Bill Egan's Christmas World. 2001. <http://christmas-world.freeservers.com/syria.html>

Energy Information Administration. "Country Analysis Briefs: Syria." U.S. Department of Energy. 3/2003. <http://www.eia.doe.gov/cabs/syria.html>

————. "Petroleum Quick Stats." U.S. Department of Energy. 2002. <http://www.eia.doe.gov/neic/quickfacts/quickoil.html>

Gordon, Michael R. "Threats and Responses: Readiness; U.S. Is Preparing Base in Gulf State to Run Iraq War." *New York Times*. 12/01/02. <http://www.nytimes.com>

Greising, David. "Saudi Women's Push for Rights No Easy Task." *Chicago Tribune*. 7/3/03. <http://www.chicagotribune.com/news/chi-0307030137jul03,0,3530410.column?coll=chi-news-hed>

Hall, Grace. "Desert Camel Spiders Create 'Urban Legends.'" Air Force Link. 7/26/02. <http://www.af.mil/news/Jul2002/n20020726_1187.shtml>

Harper, Paul. "Arab Media Go to War." *BBC News*. 3/27/03. <http://news.bbc.co.uk/2/hi/middle_east/2889441.stm>

Hawley, Caroline. "Bashar: A Year of Cautious Reform." *BBC News*. 7/17/01. <http://news.bbc.co.uk/1/hi/world/middle_east/1442526.stm>

Helou, Anissa. *Mediterranean Street Food*. New York: HarperCollins, 2002.

Hill, Don. "Saudi Arabia: For Muslims, This Is the Season of Hajj." Radio Free Europe. 2/22/01. <http://www.rferl.org/nca/features/2001/02/22022001110947.asp>

Jehl, Douglas. "Democracy's Uneasy Steps in Islamic World." *New York Times*. 11/23/01. <http://www.nytimes.com>

————. "In Changing Islamic Land, Women Savor Options." *New York Times*. 7/20/97. <http://www.nytimes.com>

———. "Tiny Gulf Emirate May Have a 200-Year Supply." *New York Times.* 7/23/97. <http://www.nytimes.com>

———. "Young Turk of the Gulf: Emir of Qatar." *New York Times.* 7/10/97. <http://www.nytimes.com>

Johnson, David. "Who Is Osama bin Laden?" Infoplease.com. 2003. <http://www.infoplease.com/spot/osamabinladen.html>

Karam, Zeina. "Syrian Kurds Speak Out for Equality." *Kurdistan Observer.* 1/11/02. <http://home.cogeco.ca/~konews/1-11-02-kurds-syria-seeking-rights.html>

King Fahd bin Abdul Aziz. "Agriculture Today." <http://www.kingfahdbinabdulaziz.com/main/j285.htm>

MacFarquhar, Neil. "Leisure Class to Working Class in Saudi Arabia." *New York Times.* 8/26/01. <http://www.nytimes.com>

Martin, Susan Taylor. "Inside Saudi Arabia: A Five-Part Special Report." *St. Petersburg Times.* 7/21/02. <http://www.sptimes.com/2002/webspecials02/saudiarabia/day1/story1.shtml>

Metz, Helen Chapin, ed. *Saudi Arabia: A Country Study.* Federal Research Division, Library of Congress. Washington, DC: Department of the Army, 1992. <http://lcweb2.loc.gov/frd/cs/satoc.html>

Microsoft Encarta Online Encyclopedia. <http://encarta.msn.com>

PBS Online. "Analysis: Wahhabism." *Frontline: Saudi Time Bomb?* <http://www.pbs.org/wgbh/pages/frontline/shows/saudi/analyses/wahhabism.html>

———. "Muhammad: Legacy of a Prophet." <http://www.pbs.org/muhammad/ma_women.shtml>

Peterson, Scott. "How Syria's Brutal Past Colors Its Future." *Christian Science Monitor.* 6/20/2000. <http://search.csmonitor.com/durable/2000/06/20/p1s3.htm>

Reuters. "Qatar's Emir Names New Crown Prince." *New York Times.* 8/05/03. <http://www.nytimes.com>

Royal Embassy of Saudi Arabia. <http://www.saudiembassy.net/>

Saudi Arabian Information Resource. <http://www.saudinf.com/main/a.htm>

Simon, Fiona. "Analysis: Syria's Economic Challenge." *BBC News.* 7/17/01. <http://news.bbc.co.uk/1/hi/world/middle_east/1443259.stm>

Smith, Craig S. "Threats and Responses: Crucial Ally; A Tiny Gulf Kingdom Bets Its Stability on Support for U.S." *New York Times.* 10/24/02. <http://www.nytimes.com>

South, Coleman. *Cultures of the World: Syria.* New York: Marshall Cavendish, 1995.

Stanley, Alessandra. "Television Review: Lessons Well Learned From the American Networks." *New York Times.* 7/10/03. <http://www.nytimes.com>

Syria Gate: All About Syria. "Christianity in Syria." 2002. <http://www.syriagate.com/Syria/about/general/christianity.htm>

Syria Ministry of Tourism. <http://www.syriatourism.org/new/index.html>

Syrian Arab Republic. Ministry of Economy and Foreign Trade. <http://www.syrecon.org/main_frame.html>

U.S. Central Intelligence Agency. *The World Factbook 2002.* <http://www.cia.gov/cia/publications/factbook/index.html>

Weiss-Armush, Anne Marie. *The Arabian Delights Cookbook.* Los Angeles: Lowell House, 1994.

Wheeler, Brian. "Al-Jazeera's Cash Crisis." *BBC News.* 4/7/03. <http://news.bbc.co.uk/2/hi/business/2908953.stm>

World Atlas.Com. "Major Landforms of the Middle East (Asia)." <http://www.worldatlas.com/webimage/countrys/melnd.htm>

CUMULATIVE INDEX

Note: Page numbers in *italics* indicate illustrations and captions.